Quality Management Systems for Assisted Reproductive Technology – ISO 9001:2000

Quality Management Systems for Assisted Reproductive Technology – ISO 9001:2000

Bryce E Carson Sr
Michael M Alper, MD
Christoph Keck, MD

Taylor & Francis
Taylor & Francis Group

LONDON AND NEW YORK

A MARTIN DUNITZ BOOK

© 2004 Taylor & Francis, an imprint of the Taylor & Francis Group

First published in the United Kingdom in 2004
by Taylor & Francis,
an imprint of the Taylor & Francis Group,
11 New Fetter Lane,
London EC4P 4EE

Tel.: +44 (0) 20 7583 9855
Fax.: +44 (0) 20 7842 2298
Website: www.tandf.co.uk

British Library Cataloguing in Publication Data

Data available on application

Library of Congress Cataloging-in-Publication Data

Data available on application

ISBN 1-84184-419-5

Distributed in North and South America by

Taylor & Francis
2000 NW Corporate Blvd
Boca Raton, FL 33431, USA

Within Continental USA
Tel.: 800 272 7737; Fax.: 800 374 3401
Outside Continental USA
Tel.: 561 994 0555; Fax.: 561 361 6018
E-mail: orders@crcpress.com

Distributed in the rest of the world by
Thomson Publishing Services
Cheriton House
North Way
Andover, Hampshire SP10 5BE, UK
Tel.: +44 (0) 1264 332424
E-mail: salesorder.tandf@thomsonpublishingservices.co.uk

Composition by Parthenon Publishing
Printed and bound in the UK by Scotprint, Haddington

Contents

Foreword   vii

Introduction   x

Chapters

1   Eight factors to creating a sustainable quality management   1
     system

2   Introduction to ISO 9001:2000   14

3   ISO 9001:2000 Clause 4 – Quality management system   20

4   ISO 9001:2000 Clause 5 – Management responsibility   46

5   ISO 9001:2000 Clause 6 – Resource management   59

6   ISO 9001:2000 Clause 7 – Product and service realization   64

7   ISO 9001:2000 Clause 8 – Measurement, analysis and   80
     improvement

Appendix

1   Comparison between ISO 9001:2000 and MBNQA   91

2   ISO 9001:2000 self-assessment instrument   96

3   Sample ISO 9001:2000 quality systems manual and   114
     procedures

4   Sample process flow charts   170

Foreword

The goal of every company and practice is to achieve a high level of professionalism and quality. This is especially true where preserving health is one of the most important values and accomplishments in our society. Providing a quality service that enhances patient satisfaction requires knowledge, exact methods, experience and innovation in diagnosis and treatment. This formula would not be complete without the responsibility, the independence and the authority of the professionals involved and their improvement efforts. Reproductive medicine is a sophisticated high-technology field with rapid scientific progress and complex disciplines utilizing formalized work processes and practices that require continual reflection. But how can you be sure that your work methods and processes develop to their maximum potential? You know what to do – but do you know how to do it? And do others within the practice?

Implementing an effective quality management system built around the concepts and core values of the ISO 9001:2000 standard supports you in this effort. The idea behind implementing an ISO 9001:2000 quality management system is quite simple: a well-organized workflow will guarantee good quality of work. Quality management is process management. You have to clarify, discuss and list these three aspects:

- What do you want to do?
- How do you want to do it?
- How can you ensure it is being done?

The ISO 9001:2000 standard provides a framework and you fill in the details – only you decide what your quality management system will look like.

The ISO 9001:2000 is a management tool that not only helps you to control the way you and your team perform your duties within the practice. It also starts the dialogue between departments and gives each member of the staff a common structure within which to grow toward individual and team accountability. What is the task of the company? What is my task within the company? Everyone is involved in the process of tracking and defining mechanisms in his domain for all the concerns, steps and procedures that never got fixed. This leads not only to a process of intensive self-surveillance but it also introduces a tool for internal supervision and advancement.

The standards in procedures and their execution are integrated into the daily work routine and its value is the implementation carried out by each staff member. The system helps you to define efficiency and competence, to pass on management information, and to solve problems effectively. ISO certification has an enormous positive effect on creativity and productivity, interpersonal understanding and team culture. Its synergy, and the identification with the aims of the company – the project 'IVF practice' – are evident. This synergy increases proportionately to the level of commitment and realization of each person involved. Establishing the ISO 9001:2000 system will lead not only to more productivity; it also leads to reduced costs. The efforts will enable everybody to focus on his client even more – the patient, the couple wanting to have a baby.

So, as you can see, ISO 9001:2000 is not just another point on the list of daunting requirements. It is more than another certification on your correspondence paper. It is a useful tool that helps you to improve your practice, regulate repeatedly performed procedures, define responsibilities, and form and integrate tests to validate the quality of work performed. The certification elements, although quite technical, are valuable tools to deliver a high-quality IVF service.

The Fertility Center Hamburg, Hamburg, Germany became certified in 1998. Rearranging our Center in that year we asked ourselves several questions: How can we improve the quality of our work? How can we improve our business practices? How can we enhance patient satisfaction? How can we strive for excellence in our IVF practice by improving pregnancy results? By discussing these and other items such as benchmarking within our team, it didn't take long to conclude that there is much more that we can do to improve.

Asking questions allowed us to learn a lot about our work and to gain an even deeper understanding of it in an unexpected way. These findings were somewhat surprising for the physicians and other experienced members of the team. The concept of a quality management system and certification allowed for the possibility to learn more about ourselves. So, as the first IVF center in Germany and as one of the first in the world, we integrated the new standard of the ISO concept into our core business and were certified in July 1998. Of course, we always tried to improve our work, to analyze our mistakes, and to do things better even before certification – like you do in your company. But the effects of the new ISO paradigms went far beyond our former efforts.

This book introduces you to the philosophy of quality management, its function and assignment – and its resulting benefits. The success of the quality management system as a new structure depends on you and your team. Dealing with it will mobilize each member of your practice and will lead to new perspectives. All your efforts will be for a good cause: more satisfied patients and more satisfaction for the people who work and care for them.

Dr Robert Fischer

Fertility Center Hamburg
Hamburg, Germany

Introduction

What is quality in assisted reproductive technologies (ART)? Is it embryo quality? Is the quality measured by the quality of the transferred embryos or by the quality of the semen? Is the quality of the ART clinic measured by the quality of the work done in the accredited laboratory? How can we ensure that all facets of the delivery of care are of the highest quality? Implementing an effective quality management system meeting ISO 9001:2000 is the answer.

What are health-care professionals saying about implementing an ISO 9001:2000 quality management system?

'Physicians here are asking what we are doing differently, because they are impressed that our service is better.' Bob Sudderith, Management Representative.

'The ISO 9000 process required a comprehensive review of departmental procedures/work instructions and operations, prompting closure of any gaps or loopholes. The ISO Certification process also decreased barriers and/or isolation between departments through the required cooperation and teamwork amongst department directors to achieve a hospital-wide goal.' Marti Miller PT MSA, Director, Department of Rehabilitation Services.

'ISO Certification affords a significant means of bringing accountability to operational systems within an organization. It serves as a pathway to improve skills and change attitudes. Implementing a quality system brings change under control, making change work for you rather than against you. System structure becomes positive opening opportunities for improvement.' Mary Lou Earnshaw, Director Medical Imaging.

'Applying this quality management system taught us to see our organization as one entity rather than a series of discrete departments – much the way our customers/patients see us.' Tom Cressy, Director Medical Records and Quality Resource Management.

'ISO has made me aware of all of the pieces of the pie – so we can give more complete quality care.' Jenny Sheppard RN, Cancer Care Center.

'Going through the ISO 9000 Certification process has taken our quality assurance program to the next level.' Rick Rybicki, Director Plant Operations, Sodexho Marriott Management Services.

'Document control, historically a nightmare in healthcare organizations, becomes systematic and organized with easy access to all that need it.' Greg Soper, Director Cardiopulmonary.

'Intense, intelligence, introspection, inspection, integrity, and *Important to Quality.*
Sweating, smart, super-system, stick together, safety and *Supports Quality.*
Organization, ordering, out-front, opportunities, ongoing = *Quality Outcomes.*' Kathy Saxton, RN, BSN Director, Obstetrics and Infection Control

There is no doubt that ISO 9000 certification has had positive outcomes for the health-care organizations that are applying the standard. The questions facing similar health-care organizations are; can we afford to apply this new quality management tool in our organization?

Health-care organizations that have been certified to ISO 9000 are evenly split between those that are accredited and those that are not. While the management system requirements outlined in the ISO 9001:2000 standard are different, the standard operates in harmony with the accreditation requirements; the ISO system ensures compliance with and brings consistency to all applicable accreditation requirements. In this case, accreditation requirements become part of the quality management system.

When an *in vitro* fertilzation (IVF) organization is not accredited by an accreditation body, the ISO standard stands alone. In summary, the question at hand may not be, 'Can we afford to apply ISO 9001:2000?' The real question is, 'Can we afford NOT to apply ISO 9001?'

The interpretive guidance to ISO 9001:2000 for IVF centers described in this book is based on the hands-on experience of the authors. The authors have extensive experience in consulting with practices. This book is intended specifically to apply to IVF programs including individuals such as nurses, ultrasonographers, administrators, laboratory personnel and physicians. It applies equally to those centers that may be private or associated with a hospital.

This book also applies to many ancillary functions such as training, research, and education, all of which can have a significant impact on patient care and outcomes.

This book is not intended to provide guidance on performance or outcome standards. The ISO 9001:2000 standard takes a systems and process approach to improving performance (practical and financial) by providing a focus on quality management, process control and quality assurance techniques to achieve planned outcomes and prevent unsatisfactory performance or non-conformance.

The examples given in this book should not be taken as prescriptive or exhaustive, or as preferred implementation methodology. There are many ways of achieving the intent of the ISO 9001:2000 standard, and the practice should adopt those approaches that best suit its mode of operation. The practice should verify that the approaches it chooses to implement provide for an effective quality management system. Each practice should identify its key processes by building on existing policies, guidelines and management control systems, in order to develop a quality management system that is suitable for, and is structured to reflect, the scope of services it supplies and the processes and specific practices it employs.

This book is an extension of Bryce's original book published for medical facilities in general. With the increasing interest of IVF centers to develop a quality management system, we developed this book specifically to assist those interested IVF centers to achieve ISO certification.

Chapter 1

Eight Factors to Creating a Sustainable Quality Management System

These eight factors were developed for use by management in order to lead their practice to improved performance.

EIGHT FACTORS TO CREATING A SUSTAINABLE QUALITY MANAGEMENT SYSTEM IN THE ASSISTED REPRODUCTIVE TECHNOLOGY CLINIC

The Eight Factors

- ᔕ Customer Focus
- 🏛 Leadership
- 👪 Involvement of People
- ( ) Process Approach
- ✖ System Approach
- ♈ Continual Improvement
- ✒ Factual Approach
- ∫ Supplier Relationship

This book has been written around the quality management principles of the ISO 9001:2000 'process' management model. The implementation of a quality management system using the process management approach espoused by the ISO 9001:2000 standard is reflective of the need for quality management in assisted reproductive technology (ART) today. The concepts defined in this book express that all clinical inputs and expected outcomes are the result of a process. In the case of a quality management system, the driving forces typically derived from the quality management system are patient/customer needs and expectations, satisfaction and continual improvement within the practice. ISO 9001:2000 suits the ART environment well because of the focus it places on the patient/customer and the emphasis it places on the IVF practice's management systems, processes, protocols and instructions. This is especially true in that an ISO 9001:2000 quality management system provides the framework and methodology for monitoring and measuring conformity to requirements, enhancing patient/customer satisfaction and continually improving the quality of service delivery. Service delivery for the IVF practice is not solely about clinical outcomes but should be the focus of every aspect of the service delivery continuum within the practice. Implementing and maintaining a sustainable quality management system becomes the way that the practice operates, always keeping its focus on the patient/customer.

The ISO 9001:2000 standard is based on eight quality management principles. These principles become the 'factors to success' for any IVF practice. These principles are customer focus, leadership, involvement of people, process approach, system approach to management, continual improvement, factual approach to decision-making, and mutually beneficial supplier relationships.

Customer focus

Since all IVF practices depend on their patients/customers, patient/customer needs both present and future should be understood and met with the aim of enhancing satisfaction. The IVF practice should strive not just to meet, but also to exceed patient/customer expectations.

Just who is the *customer*[1]? How can the infertility practice focus on the customer when it is unclear as to who the customer really is? In many practices clerical and clinical staff, administrators and other professionals struggle to understand just who the customer really is. Great is the debate that surrounds these questions, not because service deliverers are confused (they are not) but because of the complex and multi-faceted nature of the practice and the interests of different parties associated with the care delivered. Some practice administrators identify the physician as the primary customer due to the fact that the physician 'brings patients to the practice'. Clinical staff identify the patient as the primary customer as that is the population that they serve. Social workers and clergy focus on the patient and their family members' physical, emotional and spiritual needs. Billing personnel focus on payors and insurance companies as their primary customers. Risk managers and quality managers focus on collecting, collating and reporting practical

[1]*Customer*: An organization or person that receives the service. Example: Consumer, client, end-user. The customer can be either internal or external to the health-care organization. ISO 9000:2000

improvement, clinical outcomes and other data related to accreditation and regulatory bodies, and to the practice's administration and Board of Directors. The list goes on and on and so does the debate over, 'who is the customer?'

ISO 9001:2000 Clause 5.2, entitled Customer Focus requires that *Top Management*[2], 'ensure that customer requirements are determined and met with the aim of enhancing *customer satisfaction*[3]'. How can any practice truly meet this ISO 9001:2000 requirement if it has not first 'identified' its customers? It is vitally important to ensure that customers are identified so that the practice can 'enhance patient/customer satisfaction'. The identification of who customers are is the key factor to successful quality management when implementing a sustainable quality system in any practice. Administration must come together with staff to identify clearly and unambiguously the customer base, whether that base be internal or external. If the identified customer base is too narrow, then the practice will not serve all of its customers and other interested parties to the fullest of its ability.

An effective management system integrates both a system's approach and process approach to operating the IVF practice. Because all personnel within the practice are critical and essential in carrying out the practice's mission, goals, objectives and vision, then all customers must be identified to ensure effective quality management.

Leadership

Leaders within the IVF center establish unity of purpose, cast vision, provide direction, and create an internal environment within the practice where employees can work to their fullest potential. Leadership within the practice creates an environment in which all staff and employees can become fully involved in achieving the practice's mission, vision, goals and objectives. Leadership is the ability to influence individuals or groups toward the achievement of goals. Leadership, as a process, shapes the goals of a group or organization, motivates behavior toward the achievement of those goals, and helps define group or organizational culture. It is primarily a process of influence. Leadership is a

---

[2]*Top Management*: A person or group of persons who directs and controls the organization at the highest level. ISO 9000:2000

[3]*Customer Satisfaction*: The customer's perception of the degree to which the customer's requirements have been fulfilled. Comment: Customer complaints are an indicator of low customer satisfaction but their absence does not necessarily imply high customer satisfaction. Even when all of the customer's requirements have been agreed and fulfilled this does not assure high customer satisfaction. ISO 9000:2000

dynamic or changing process in the sense that, while influence is always present, the persons exercising that influence may change.

Because influence is essential, the traditional leadership methodology of controlling, dictating and prescribing how work will be accomplished, commanding and telling employees what to do expecting obedience, judging and sizing up employees' performance, delving out rewards and punishments and guarding turf and hording resources is still alive and well throughout many practices. Such leadership tactics cause practices to become dysfunctional – new methods MUST be nurtured.

The new leadership paradigm is very slow at gaining understanding. Administrators and managers within IVF centers and practices must understand and participate in high-involvement leadership. As high-involvement leadership takes hold, the dysfunctional methods described above will become obsolete. Roles that facilitate high-involvement leadership must take hold. Following are examples of how to facilitate high-involvement leadership. High-involvement leaders:

(1) *Discover new ways*   Leadership must enforce the 'one best way' of working when necessary. As processes are defined it is equally as important to know where flexibility and creative problem solving are not only possible but demanded, as it is to define the required process steps that must by their definition be adhered to at all times. ISO 9001:2000 requires the practice to determine the sequence and interactions of its processes in order to facilitate change and bring about improvement. Leaders must encourage and empower direct reports and other interested parties to bring forth 'best process practice' ideas. Lastly, leaders must seek new and better ways of accomplishing the mission; leaders must be visionary.

(2) *Make the path clear*   In contrast to traditional leaders the high-involvement leader illuminates and lights the path where the practice should be headed. Notice that this type of leader lights up the path and does not use a spotlight in order to see miles ahead. The leader leads the practice in small steps with the knowledge and vision of what lies ahead in the darkness.

(3) *Encourage others along the way*   Implementing ISO 9001:2000 requires that the leader assume some degree of risk. This added risk requires employees also to assume risk and added responsibility. The high-involvement leader needs to be vocal in their support of the ISO 9001:2000 initiative and not only talk about the process but become actively involved and visible throughout the project.

Encouragement is needed in order to keep the project on-track and to ensure that people understand the importance of implementing a sustainable quality management system.

ⴕⴕⴕ　Involvement of people

Every IVF practice is comprised of people/employees. Employee involvement is creating an environment in which people have an impact on decisions and actions that affect their jobs. Employee involvement is not the goal nor is it a tool, as practiced in many organizations. Rather, it is a management and leadership philosophy about how people are most enabled to contribute to continuous improvement and the on-going success of the IVF practice. The practice must involve people as much as possible in all aspects of work decisions and planning. This involvement increases ownership and commitment, retains the practice's best employees, and fosters an environment in which people choose to be motivated and contributing.

How to involve employees in decision-making and continuous improvement activities is the strategic aspect of involvement and can include such methods as suggestion systems, work teams, continuous improvement meetings, Kaizen (the relentless pursuit for doing things a better way) events, corrective and preventive action processes, and periodic discussions with supervisors.

Intrinsic to most employee involvement processes is training in team effectiveness, communication and problem solving; the development of reward and recognition systems; and, frequently, the sharing of gains made through employee involvement efforts.

For people and organizations who desire a model to apply, the best I have discovered was developed from work by Tannenbaum and Schmidt (1958)[4]. They provide a continuum for leadership and involvement that includes an increasing role for employees and a decreasing role for supervisors in the decision process. The continuum includes this progression:

> *Tell*　The supervisor makes the decision and announces it to staff. The supervisor provides complete direction. This method is useful when communicating about safety issues, government regulations, decisions that neither require nor ask for employee input.

> *Sell*　The supervisor makes the decision and then attempts to gain commitment from staff by 'selling' the positive aspects of the

[4]Tannenbaum R, Schmidt W. How to choose a leadership pattern. *Harvard Business Review*, 1958;36:95–101

decision. This method is useful when employee commitment is needed, but the decision is not open to employee influence.

Consult The supervisor invites input into a decision while retaining authority to make the final decision himself. The key to a successful consultation is to inform employees, on the front end of the discussion, that their input is needed, but that the supervisor is retaining the authority to make the final decision. This is the level of involvement that can create employee dissatisfaction most readily when this is not clear to the people providing input.

Join The supervisor invites employees to make the decision with the supervisor. The supervisor considers his voice equal in the decision process. The key to a successful join is when the supervisor truly builds consensus around a decision and is willing to keep his influence equal to that of the others providing input.

Improvement of personnel within the practice achieves maximum benefit when everyone is fully involved, using their abilities to the practice's advantage. As leadership lights up and illuminates the direction as to where the practice is headed, people will begin to understand the importance of their role within the practice only after they begin to see how implementation of ISO 9001:2000 can create a positive effect and impact upon their jobs. An effectively implemented ISO 9001:2000 management system should make everyone's jobs easier to perform and less redundant. When personnel realize the positive benefit that ISO 9001:2000 quality management systems has for them personally, people will become more intimately involved in identifying methods for improving the processes they own.

()   Process approach

A business process is any broad collection of activities within the practice that is involved in the ultimate goal of carrying out IVF treatment to the customer. Practice and clinical processes are typically evaluated from the customer's viewpoint. Ensuring a smoothly running practice/clinical process is critical in maximizing the added value provided to its customers. Managing the key processes efficiently is critical to the success of the practice/clinic. But managing those processes is harder than it may seem at first – mostly because these processes do not stand alone, but interact with one another.

There are many types of clinical processes such as key processes, support processes and sub-processes. Typical ART/IVF processes include:

Procurement   Securing materials and equipment used in carrying out clinical and non-clinical services to patients and other interested parties.

Clinical development   Planning new methods, practices, protocols or services for patients/customers or refining existing methods, practices, protocols or services.

Clinical activities   Creating the methods, practices, protocols or services for patients/customers.

Service delivery   Scheduling and providing services to patients/customers.

Customer support   Providing assistance to patients/customers after they have purchased the product or service.

The more that the practice/clinic looks and the sequence and interaction of its processes the further it goes in improving the way it delivers services to its patients/customers. To ensure continuous, successful process development and improvement take into consideration the following important key issues.

Targets should be clear and measurable ensuring a strong commitment from management and practice/clinical personnel. Clinical/practice personnel are a valuable source of information. Involvement of people greatly assists in creating the commitment and ensuring the acceptance of proposed process changes. Communication is what helps create involvement, commitment and target setting.

Building a process-oriented model (shown below) can solve many problems that are hidden from a traditional functional viewpoint. A process model is designed to help all the people involved understand the whole picture and their part in it. Building such a model requires teamwork, to ensure that all available knowledge is used in the model. A basic model can consist of things such as specific activi-

Activity	Benefit	Potential
Manage	• Manage performance and continuous improvements	
Improve	• Execute actions to improve lead times, optimize resources, etc	
Measure & simulate	• Identify costs, lead time, quality, cost for non-value-adding activities, improvement potential, problem areas	
Document	• Improved routines, securing of quality	
Identify	• Increased understanding, involvement, ideas	

ties, process steps, organizational functions, information and material. The model can also contain notes about potential problems in the business process, ideas for improvement and other comments.

Quality documentation is an important part of business process management. Flow-charting work practice and work-flow is an excellent way of identifying the sequence and interaction of processes within the practice/clinic. Documenting all the processes within the practice/clinic aids in communication throughout the organization. The greatest challenge in the practice/clinic is to keep the documentation up-to-date and accessible to those involved. A great help in keeping the documentation up-to-date is to use the practice/clinic's Intranet.

The greatest advantage of the process approach is that it helps in understanding how things are really done in the organization, revealing problems, bottlenecks and inefficiencies that could remain hidden in a typical organization that is on the face of it functioning normally. The process approach also helps you:

- Reduce lead times

- Decrease costs

- Improve internal efficiency

- Improve overall quality

- Increase patient/customer and employee satisfaction

Process orientation and process thinking contributes to a better understanding of the ultimate goal and output of the clinic/practice and the individual employee's role in it. However, most important is the notion that the clinical/practice management processes and practices and their resulting output is the real interface with the organization's customers – not just individual functions of the organization. Process modeling and the effective analysis of business processes enables the clinic/practice to develop a highly effective organization and improve its effectiveness and quality of work with the aim of enhancing customer satisfaction.

It should be the ultimate goal of the IVF center to achieve the highest degree of efficiency when related resources and practice and clinical activities are managed together as a process. Figure 1.1 demonstrates the ISO 9000 process management model (developed from ISO 9001:2000) of continual process improvement. As stated above resources and activities must be managed as a process. Simply put, a process is defined as the steps and actions necessary for transforming inputs into outputs. The output from one process often forms the input for another.

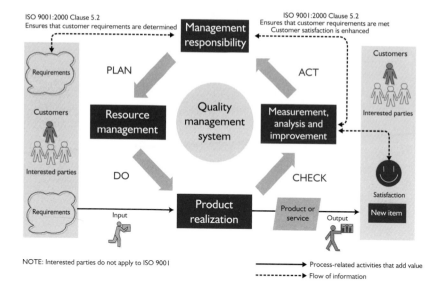

Figure 1.1   Continual improvement of the quality management system

Let's look at one example. A patient is discharged from her egg retrieval surgery and admitted to the nursing unit. The patients chart (the process input document) is delivered to the nursing unit. The nursing unit delivers the required care to the patient (the delivery of care process). The patient is provided post-surgery education and subsequently discharged (the process output – process completed).

The medical record/chart (the coding process input document) is forwarded to coding department. The coding department completes coding and the medical record/chart (the coding process output – process completed) is forwarded to the records department.

The medical records department receives the medical record/chart (medical records process input), checks, logs and records (process) and files the record/chart (medical records process output – process complete).

Clinical/practice leadership must develop a process approach when managing the IVF practice's systems. Processes need to be defined and documented in order to understand more clearly the process flow of work. Once process flow is understood, improvements can be made when variation in process is identified and change is found necessary. Understanding and documenting the process flow of work also provides new employees with the opportunity to learn their jobs more quickly thereby limiting the number of errors made.

✄ System approach to management

IVF practices should identify, understand and manage a system of inter-related processes for a given objective. While processes are documented as a function of the process approach, these processes must be managed as a complete holistic system. These clinical/practice processes must contribute to the effectiveness and efficiency of the organization. The system approach to management must take into account the following:

- Determining the needs and expectations of the patient/customer

- Establishing a quality policy

- Establishing goals and objectives

- Determining the processes necessary to achieve the objectives

- Establishing measures for the effectiveness of each process toward achieving the objectives

- Applying the measures to determine current effectiveness

- Determining methods of preventing non-conformities

- Looking for ways to improve

- Prioritizing those improvements

- Planning strategies, processes and resources to deliver improvements

- Implementing the plan

- Monitoring the effects

- Assessing the results

- Reviewing the improvement activities to determine appropriate follow-up actions

The system approach is a different approach at a fundamental level. For example, if a laboratory specimen is lost, the system approach would be to investigate how the system and its process of controls for that activity allowed such an error, rather than deciding who slipped up. Process problem solving now is effective for the entire process instead of focusing on individual employee actions.

♛ Continual improvement

This is a permanent objective of any practice/clinic. IVF centers must focus attention, time and effort on meeting patient/customer needs and meeting patient expectations. As stated under customer focus, the practice must know who the customer is, thereby turning their needs and expectations into requirements, establishing processes for soliciting customer feedback, developing indicators, measuring and monitoring processes and service delivery and using the information to plan and execute effective corrective and preventive action in a timely manner.

Clinics and practices large and small are expected continually to improve their processes and practices. The continual improvement philosophy espoused by ISO 9001:2000 creates an important impact on customer satisfaction, satisfaction of other interested parties, profitability and longevity of the organization. Leadership's commitment and active participation is essential to the success of continual improvement processes. Any activity that is repeated can be improved. A suggestion for improvement is not a statement of failure in the past, but of improvement for the future.

☞ Factual approach to decision-making

The IVF center must base decisions on the logical or intuitive analysis of data and information. While the goal must obviously be zero errors, data creates real perspective instead of an emotional response. Developing a fact-based approach to decision-making is both a cultural and clinical/practice-wide process issue. As with any organizational priority, top management needs to drive the transition. Many top clinics/practices use fact-based organizational analysis as a source of competitive advantage. By developing organizational processes for identifying and considering key clinical, business and other outcome data, these practices/clinics are able to make higher-quality decisions. In the long-term, this contributes to measurable business and clinical success.

To understand the true value of fact-based approaches to business and clinical decision-making, it is helpful to understand examples of how this approach can strengthen the IVF clinic/practice's business approach. Basically, making a commitment to collecting and integrating key business and clinical data into decision-making ensures that the organization's key constituencies are best served.

Patients/customers are provided relevant, competitive medical products and services. Employees contribute to moving organizational goals and objectives in a direct and timely manner. Shareholders, owners and

Boards of Directors recognize that the clinic/practice understands key issues and is poised to exploit opportunity. Typically, there are three categories of organizations that lack a fact-based approach to clinical outcomes, business analysis and decision-making.

There are *uninformed* clinics/practices who do not know that they should be collecting and integrating external and internal data into planning and decision-making. These organizations do not understand that good marketing is based on fact and that effective business and marketing strategy is mandatory to be successful. The *frugal* clinics/practices are those that would like to be fact-based but lack the motivation to invest in proper decision-based processes. The *biased* clinics/practices skew business and marketing facts, and introduce bias into their strategic and tactical plans.

To the customers, competitors and the outside world, a clinic/practice's business strategy is communicated through its marketing message and strategic partnerships. All decisions within the clinic/practice must be based on realistic and meaningful facts.

§   Mutually beneficial supplier relationships

These require that purchasing relationships between the clinic/practice and its suppliers be structured in such a way as to benefit and enhance the ability of the organization and its suppliers/physicians/subcontractors to create value for its patients/customers.

SUMMARY

ISO 9001:2000 organizes these eight principles into five clauses. When an IVF practice is audited for compliance, implementation of all ISO 9001:2000 quality management system requirements must be evaluated. These five quality management system standards are:

Clause 4   Quality management system requirements;

Clause 5   Management responsibility (leadership);

Clause 6   Resource management (people, facilities, equipment);

Clause 7   Service realization (process identification and process management);

Clause 8   Measurement analysis and improvement (improvement for patient/customer satisfaction).

These five clauses describe what clinics/practices must accomplish and implement in order to provide quality services to patients/customers. The process management philosophy of the ISO 9001:2000 standard (see Figure 1.1) begins its focus on the customer/patient and their requirements; everything to do with quality starts and ends with the customer/patient. What the customer/patient wants, needs and expects becomes the input to the quality management system. This input then feeds into the service planning process and finally into requirements for service delivery. Management responsibility (leadership), resource management (people, facilities and equipment), product realization (process) and measurement analysis and improvement (improvement for customer/patient satisfaction) describe what practices must do to deliver quality services.

The actual delivery of service becomes the clinic/practice's service output. The practice is then required to evaluate pertinent information on customer/patient satisfaction and/or dissatisfaction. This can be accomplished through implementing ISO 9001:2000 Clause 8, Measurement, Analysis and Improvement. Measurements and evaluations become feedback on the practice's ability to meet customer/patient requirements. The clinic/practice is required to measure and monitor both service delivery processes and the service delivery itself. Satisfaction measures are used as feedback to evaluate and validate whether customer/patient requirements have been met.

Chapter 2

Introduction to ISO 9001:2000

Practical processes remain static until we write down what we do. Only then do we truly understand what really happens. True change can then take place.

INTRODUCTION

What is ISO? Most practices find ISO to be an acronym of Greek origin. In fact it is just that! It is Greek for 'all sides being equal'. The ISO standards were derived to ensure uniformity and harmonization of standards that have proliferated around the world. The ISO 9000 series (ISO 9000:2000, ISO 9001:2000 and ISO 9004:2000) are quality management system standards that are applied generically and apply to any and all practices.

The ISO 9000 series standards define the minimum requirements that a practice must meet to assure their customers of acceptable service that meets their internal requirements and established outcomes. ISO 9000 has become the international language of quality. Since it was issued in 1987, the ISO 9000 series of quality system standards has been used more and more throughout Europe, the USA and other parts of the world as the standard for quality system registration. Indeed, there is practically unanimous worldwide acceptance of these standards as quality system standards.

ISO (International Standardization Organization) is headquartered in Geneva, Switzerland. Notice that 'ISO' does not mean International Standards Practice. There are over 120 countries worldwide that are members of the International Practice for Standardization. Government or quasi-government entities represent member countries. These member countries have adopted the ISO 9000 series as their country's national standard for quality management systems. In the United States the government agency responsible for issuance of national standards is the US Department of Commerce through the American National Standards Institute (ANSI), the ISO representative in the United States. ANSI has published the US equivalent version of the ISO 9000 series that is known as *ANSI/ISO/ASQ Q9000, Q9001 and Q9004*[5]. These documents are equivalent to the international version of ISO 9000, 9001 and 9004.

ISO 9000 SERIES (ISO 9000, ISO 9001 AND ISO 9004)

In 1987, the first ISO 9000 series standards were issued. In 1994, the standards were revised for the first time. The 1994 revisions had minimal impact on registered practices regarding their ability to implement the revisions. In 1997, discussion began regarding a 2000 revision to the standards. The committees given the task of investigating a revision conducted a global survey of users of the ISO standards. In 1997, a large global survey of 1120 ISO 9000 users and customers was conducted to understand their needs more clearly. This was accomplished using a questionnaire covering:

+ Attitudes towards the existing standards

+ Requirements for the revised standards

+ The relationship between the quality management system standards and the environmental management system standards

The following significant user and customer needs were determined from the analysis of these questionnaires:

+ The revised standards should be simple to use, easy to understand, and use clear language and terminology

+ The revised standards should have a common structure based on a process model

---

[5]Standards can be purchased from ASQ Quality Press, P.O. Box 3005, Milwaukee, WI 53201. Tel: 800-248-1946

- ISO 9001 requirements should include demonstration of continuous improvement and prevention of non-conformity

- The revised standards should be suitable for all sizes of practices, operating in any economic or industrial sector, and the manufacturing orientation of the current standards should be removed

- Provision should be made for the exclusion of requirements that do not apply to a practice

- The revised standards should facilitate self-evaluation

- The revised standards should have increased compatibility with the ISO 14000 series of Environmental Management System Standards

- ISO 9001 should address effectiveness while ISO 9004 should address both efficiency and effectiveness

- ISO 9004 should help achieve benefits for all interested parties, i.e. customers, owners, employees, suppliers and society

To ensure that the revised standards satisfy these user and customer needs, a validation process was implemented. The validation process allowed for direct feedback from users and customers at key milestones during the revision process to determine how well these needs were met and to identify opportunities for improvement.

RE-STRUCTURING AND CONSOLIDATION OF THE ISO 9000 FAMILY OF STANDARDS

Up to the year 2000, the ISO 9000 family of standards contained some 20+ standards and related documents. This proliferation of quality system-type standards had been a particular concern of ISO 9000 users and customers because the original intent for creating an international standard was to produce a single standard to be used by all. To respond to this concern, the ISO committee agreed that in the year 2000 the ISO 9000 family of

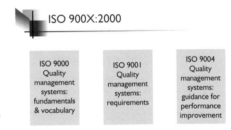

standards would consist of three primary standards supported by a number of technical reports. As far as possible, the key points in the former 20 standards were integrated into the three primary standards. The generic nature of the standards allows sector needs to be addressed without additional guidelines.

The three primary standards are:

ISO 9000:2000   Quality management systems – Fundamentals and vocabulary

ISO 9001:2000   Quality management systems – Requirements

ISO 9004:2000   Quality management systems – Guidelines for performance improvements

ISO 9000:2000

The current ISO 8402 Quality vocabulary standard was revised to become the ISO 9000:2000 standard. This standard includes an introduction to quality fundamentals and concepts, as well as a revised vocabulary or glossary of terms.

ISO 9001 and ISO 9004:2000

The 1994 versions of ISO 9001, ISO 9002 and ISO 9003 standards are consolidated into the single revised ISO 9001 standard. The revised ISO 9001 and ISO 9004 standards were developed as a 'consistent pair' of standards. Whereas the revised ISO 9001 more clearly addresses the quality management system requirements for a practice to demonstrate its capability to meet customer requirements, the revised ISO 9004 standard is intended to lead beyond the mere implementation of ISO 9001 towards the development of a comprehensive quality management system. In particular, the revised ISO 9004 is not an implementation guide for ISO 9001 implementation.

Tailoring of the ISO 9001 requirements is permitted to omit requirements that do not apply to a practice. Tailoring may be used by those

practices that would seek registration to ISO 9002 or ISO 9003 under the 1994 standards.

The revised ISO 9001 and ISO 9004 standards have been developed using a simple process-based structure. This is a departure from the old ISO 9000 1994, 20-element structure and adopts the process management approach widely used in practices today. Also, the new process-based structure is consistent with the Plan-Do-Check-Act improvement cycle. The major clause titles in the revised standards are:

Structure of the ISO 9001 Standard

23 Pages

0 Introduction
1 Scope
2 Normative reference
3 Terms and definitions
4 Quality management system
5 Management responsibilty
6 Resource management
7 Product realization
8 Measurement, analysis and improvement

- *Clause 4*   Quality management system (e.g. process management, documentation, records)

- *Clause 5*   Management responsibility (e.g. policy, objectives, planning, responsibility and authority, documentation, communications and management review)

- *Clause 6*   Resource management (e.g. human resources, infrastructure and work environment)

- *Clause 7*   Product realization (e.g. customer requirements, design, purchasing, production and service operations, and calibration)

- *Clause 8*   Measurement, analysis and improvement (e.g. audit, satisfaction, inspection and testing, non-conformity, corrective and preventive action and continuous improvement)

Since Figure 1.1 in Chapter 1 is a model of the complete quality system processes, it is capable of demonstrating both vertical and horizontal process integration in a closed-loop manner (see Figure 1.1).

For a vertical loop example, management defines requirements under Management responsibility; necessary resources are determined and applied within Resource management; processes are established and implemented under Product realization; results are measured, analyzed and improved through Measurement, analysis and improvement.

Management review closes the loop, as the cycle returns to Management responsibility for change authorization and initiation of improvement.

As an example of a major horizontal loop, the model recognizes the fact that customers play a significant role during the process of input of needs and requirements; the identified product realization processes are then exercised and customer satisfaction is evaluated at process output. Output data are used to improve the customer inputs, completing the closure of the horizontal process loop.

A local loop may be encountered, for example, where a product or service is checked, feedback given to those directly involved in the operation, and where necessary action is taken on problems encountered.

Chapter 3

ISO 9001:2000 Clause 4 – Quality Management System

The system approach to management: practices should identify, understand and manage a system of interrelated processes for a given objective.

The ISO 9001:2000 standard is 23 pages in length and is further broken into eight sections. These sections are known as clauses. Each 'clause' is further defined by 'sub-clauses'. These clauses and sub-clauses contain the actual quality management system requirements of the ISO 9001:2000 standard. Chapters 3–7 of this book discuss each of the ISO 9001:2000 clause requirements in detail and describe how the practice should implement the requirements.

CLAUSES 0–2: SCOPE, NORMATIVE REFERENCES AND DEFINITIONS

These three clauses of the ISO 9001:2000 standard contain basic information that an IVF center needs to be aware of, and are usually not a part of the actual implementation of the quality management system, even though they are a part of the ISO 9001:2000 standard itself.

CLAUSE 3: TERMS AND DEFINITIONS

Prior to providing an explanation of the ISO 9001:2000 requirements, we must look at some of the terms and explanatory notes regarding some aspects of ISO 9001. As with all new things, there needs to be a basic understanding of vocabulary. As previously stated, the ISO 9000:2000 standard includes various terms and definitions. Additionally, there are a few terms and definitions found within the ISO 9001:2000 document that personnel first need to understand before effective

Terminology

Terms
- Top Management
- Organization
- Suppliers
- Monitoring
- Product Realization
- Customer Satisfaction
- Review Input and Review Output

implementation of a quality management system can be carried out. The notes that follow need to be read in conjunction with the relevant sections of ISO 9001:2000.

Product: the result of a process

Note 1   There are four generic product categories, as follows:

- Services (e.g. embryo freezing IVF)

- Software (e.g. computer program, website)

- Hardware (e.g. laboratory pipette)

- Processed materials (e.g. media)

Many products/services comprise elements belonging to different generic product/service categories. Whether the product is called service, software, hardware or processed material depends on the dominant element. For example, the offered product 'automobile' consists of hardware (e.g. tires), processed materials (e.g. fuel, cooling liquid), software (e.g. engine control software, driver's manual) and service (e.g. operating explanations given by the salesman).

Note 2   Service is the result of at least one activity necessarily performed at the interface between the IVF center and customer and is generally intangible. Provision of a service can involve, for example, the following:

- An activity performed on a customer-supplied tangible product (e.g. sperm washing for intrauterine insemination)

- An activity performed on a customer-supplied intangible product (e.g. decision of drug dosage after reviewing ultrasound and blood test)

- The delivery of an intangible product (e.g knowledge about the IVF procedure)

- The creation of ambience for the customer (e.g. in doctor's waiting room)

Software consists of information and is generally intangible and can be in the form of approaches, transactions or procedures.

Hardware is generally tangible and its amount is a countable characteristic. Processed materials are generally tangible and their amount is a continuous characteristic. Hardware and processed materials are often referred to as goods.

Note 3   Quality assurance is mainly focused on the intended product or on the service.

Fertility service delivery

Results of documented or non-documented activities generated at the interface between the IVF center and the customer and by the center's internal activities which meet the customer's holistic needs; the services provided are the result of planned activities; the IVF practice or the customer may be represented at the interface by family members, friends, personnel or medical equipment; the customer's activities at the interface with the practice may be essential to the service delivery.

Process

Set of interrelated or interacting activities that transform inputs into outputs.

Note 1   Inputs to a process are generally outputs of other processes.

Note 2   Processes in a practice are generally planned and carried out under controlled conditions to add value.

Note 3   A process where the conformity of the resulting product cannot be readily or economically verified is frequently referred to as a 'special process'.

System

Set of interrelated or interacting elements.

Customer

Practice or person that receives the product. This implementation book uses the term 'patient and/or customer' to describe patients and other customers or clients of a practice. The term 'customer', as used in ISO 9001:2000, can imply any or all of the following, as appropriate in the context:

- A patient

- A patient's family

- The patient's referring doctor

- A surgeon, specialist, visiting medical officer, allied health professional or other practice

- A company or practice with whom a contract to provide a service is entered into

- A government department

- Fund

- Another provider

- An internal customer (i.e. within the practice's own practice), or a relevant society or community group

Customer property

Products/patient belongings/personal effects that require a special degree of handling, care and maintenance; products/belongings that the customer provides to the IVF practice, which will be returned to the customer or the customer's designee at some agreed upon time or at the completion of the service provided or used in the delivery of care; examples of customer supplied product belongings are frozen embryos and frozen sperm, which will be returned to the patient.

Non-conformity

Non-fulfillment of a specified requirement. Reporting of non-conformities may be recorded on Incident Reports or Occurrence Reports or a combination of both (e.g. needle pricks, patient injuries, failure to administer medication, wrong medications, patient falls, etc.) The definition of 'non-conformity' covers the absence of one or more process characteristics, specified or obligatory requirements, or management system requirements, i.e. an unsatisfactory outcome or failure in a particular service to a patient/customer, or a failure to comply with an established quality management system and other procedures. (See ISO 9001:2000 Clause 8.3.)

Review of customer requirements

Planned and systematic activities (e.g. administration of anesthesia, doctors contracts to provide services, etc.) carried out by the fertility service practice before signing the 'contract' in order to assure that all requirements for service are adequately defined and are free from ambiguity, documented and can be realized by the practice. 'Contract' reviews can be carried out jointly with the customer/patient and can be repeated at various stages during the delivery continuum.

Medical record

The account compiled by physicians and other professionals of a patient's medical history, present illness, findings on examination, details of treatment, and notes on progress. The medical record is the legal record of care[6].

Medical policies and procedures

The act, method or manner of proceeding in some process or course of action; a particular cause of action by way of doing something, such as policies and procedures governing the medical staff credentialing process.

CLAUSE 4.1: GENERAL REQUIREMENTS

The requirements for fertility services must be clearly defined by the practice. Many different service delivery processes are involved within the operation of any facility. These varied processes that deliver the service should be defined in terms of specific service characteristics or deliverables. These service deliverables or characteristics may not always be observable to the customer, but they may affect service delivery performance. A fertility center's service deliverables or characteristics may be quantitative (measurable) or qualitative (comparable), for example:

- The IVF center's physical plant, number of personnel and quality of materials

- Waiting time, delivery time of service and processing time

---

[6]*Joint Commission on Accreditation of Healthcare Organizations (JCAHO) definition*

- Safety, reliability and security

- Responsiveness, accessibility, courtesy comfort, aesthetics of the environment, competence, dependability, accuracy, completeness, state of the art, credibility, and effective communication.

All processes that are used to deliver these services must be controlled. Because of the nature of our services, remedial (corrective) action is sometimes possible during the actual delivery of the service. It is usually not possible to rely on 'final inspection' to influence service quality at the customer interface where customers or patients may assess non-conforming conditions.

The delivery of services is a highly personalized one. The more definable and controlled the *process* is, the greater the opportunity to apply structured and disciplined quality system principles.

The examples given in this book should not be taken as prescriptive or exhaustive, or as a preferred implementation methodology. There are many ways of achieving the intent of the ISO 9001:2000 standard, and the IVF practice should adopt those approaches that best suit its mode of operation. The practice should verify that the implementation approaches defined in this book provide for an effective quality management system. Each practice should identify its key processes by building on its existing policies and procedures and management and control systems, in order to develop a quality management system that is suitable for, and is structured to reflect, the scope of services it supplies and the processes and specific practices it employs.

> **IMPLEMENTATION GUIDANCE NOTE:** As a practice there may be some issues or problems in reconciling the differences between what a patient/customer may perceive as an expectation and what the IVF center can actually deliver by way of treatment or a care program. For example, a patient may *expect* that she will conceive with IVF but the doctor realizes that egg donation will probably be necessary.

CLAUSE 4.2: DOCUMENTATION REQUIREMENTS

A review of the new international standard indicates that the requirement for documenting quality system procedures for each standard is conspicuously absent. The ISO 9001:2000 standard in Clause 4.2 Documentation Requirements, states that:

'The quality management system documentation shall include:

(a)   documented statements of a quality policy and quality objectives;

(b)   a quality manual;

(c)   documented procedures[7] required in this International Standard;

(d)   documents needed by the practice to ensure the effective operation and control of its processes;

(e)   records required by this International Standard.'

When establishing a quality management system there are two primary types of documents that the practice must create:

(1) *Documented proce-dures required by the ISO 9001:2000 standard;*

(2) *Documents required by the practice.*

The   ISO   9001:2000 standard specifically re-quires that certain mandatory procedures be written. The following procedures are required to be 'established, documented, implemented and maintained':

Element 4 – Quality Management System

- We have to have procedures
- Some for the whole system, that say how the system works
- Some that say what is the order of steps and who needs to work together to meet our customers' needs
- Work instructions that tell the details when we need them

- Clause 4.2.3   Control of documents

- Clause 4.2.4   Control of quality records

- Clause 8.2.2   Internal audits

- Clause 8.3   Control of non-conformity

- Clause 8.5.2   Corrective action

- Clause 8.5.3   Preventive action

---

[7]Where the term 'documented procedure' appears within the ISO 9001:2000 standard, this requires the procedure to be established, documented, implemented and maintained...

Note These are the only clauses of the ISO 9001:2000 standard where a 'documented procedure' is required.

The ISO 9001:2000 standard provides the IVF center with some flexibility in establishing its quality management system documentation by indicating that these 'documented procedures' will depend upon the particular size and type of services that the practice provides, the complexity and actions and interactions of the processes being carried out and the competency of the personnel. Remember, wherever the standard refers to the words 'documented procedure' it is expected that a corresponding documented approach will be provided as to how the activity or process is to be carried out.

Clause 4.2d of the ISO 9001:2000 standard uses the term 'documents'[8] to identify how the practice will provide the information that people need to perform and carry out the activities (processes). The term 'documents' is intended to provide a less onerous requirement on the practice. The standard allows the practice to 'document', in any form or method desired, the explanation of the order and interaction of the processes being used to ensure that the product and/or services offered meet the specified requirements.

This does not necessarily mean that processes themselves be written down or covered by 'documents', it is just a description of how they are expected to relate to each other. It may be necessary for the Center to describe how some of the practices and processes are undertaken in order to carry out the process and what controls are placed on the process. Remember, documents can be in any form and may vary enormously from formal documents: from technical notes incorporated into a drawing to an equipment instruction manual. Documents may also be in pictorial or video form or may be of an external nature. They may also take the form of a model or sample, documents held on computer hard disks, diskettes or CD-ROM, audiotapes or graphic posters. The choice is yours.

Both 'documented procedures' and 'documents' should indicate, to the extent necessary, who does what, where, when, why and how. Excessive detail in procedures and other documents does not necessarily ensure more control over the process, practice or activity. In fact, excessive detail should be avoided at all costs unless it provides value to

---

[8]*Documents*: Information and its supporting medium; for example, a 'document' is defined as, but not limited to, a record, specification, procedure document, drawing, report or standard. A set of documents, for example, including specifications and records, is frequently called 'documentation'.

The supporting medium can be paper, magnetic, electronic or optical computer disk, photograph or master sample, or a combination thereof.

the process, practice or activity. Training of personnel and the necessary job skills to carry out the activity may reduce the need for overly detailed process control documents, provided everyone conducting the process or carrying out the activity has the information they need to do their job correctly.

It is essential when installing an effective ISO 9001:2000 quality management system within the practice to begin with the applicable ISO 9001:2000 'requirements'[9]. Most practices begin their work creating ISO 9001:2000 documentation *before* they really understand what is needed and end up with far more documentation than the ISO 9001:2000 standard requires. The ISO 9001:2000 standard 'requirements' make reference to various plans, procedures, instructions and the types of information described in the chart below.

All of the ISO 9001:2000 'requirements' describe information that must be recorded, provided, documented, measured, monitored, reviewed, etc. but only *one* requirement (ISO 9001:2000 Clause 4.2

ISO 9001:2000 requirement	Required information
Clause 4. Quality Management System	Quality policy and objectives, statements, quality manual, procedures, records, *requirements*.
Clause 5. Management Responsibility	Statutory and regulatory *requirements*, quality policy and objectives, *requirements*, plans, review inputs and outputs, customer feedback, results.
Clause 6. Resource Management	*Requirements*, records, procedures and results.
Clause 7. Product Realization	Plans, *requirements*, objectives, data, product information, contracts, inquiries, orders, statutory, regulatory and other *requirements*, criteria, records, work instructions, data.
Clause 8. Measurement Analysis and Improvement	Plans, procedures, results, planned arrangements, measurements, data, *requirements*.

[9]*Requirements*: Need or expectation that is stated, generally implied or obligatory.

Documentation Requirements) defines the required methodology for organizing and managing the practice's documented quality management system.

Top management should define the documentation only deemed necessary and needed to support effective and efficient processes and operations. ISO 9001:2000 requirements state that the quality management system must be established, documented, implemented and maintained. The term 'documented' can be interpreted as meaning recorded in some manner (i.e. computer, hard copy, online, video taped, etc.).

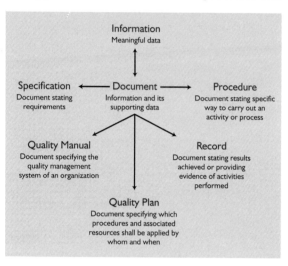

CLAUSE 4.2.1a: QUALITY POLICY, GOALS AND OBJECTIVES

The first piece of documentation that needs to be created within the IVF center's quality management system is the documented statements of a quality policy and quality objectives. Practice goals and objectives are identified and documented in support of the 'quality policy'. Many practices already have mission and vision statements in place and may use these statements in lieu of creating a new statement called a 'quality policy'. For those IVF units that have not established a mission or vision statement a 'quality policy' will have to be established by top management and documented. Objectives for meeting the quality policy must also be documented. Remember, when identifying and creating practical goals and objectives, they must be... S.M.A.R.T.!

Specific Measurable Attainable Reasonable and Timely.

When establishing and documenting objectives, top management should consider such things as the practice's current and future business needs, product and/or service and process performance, current satisfaction of customers and resources needed to meet the planned objectives.

CLAUSES 4.2.1b AND 4.2.2: THE QUALITY MANUAL

ISO 9001:2000 Clause 4.2b and Clause 4.2.2 require that a *quality manual*[10] be established and maintained. A quality manual is a document that provides consistent information, both internally and externally, about the practice's quality management system.

The quality manual must include:

(1) The scope of the quality management system;

(2) Documented procedures or reference to them;

(3) A description of the interaction between the processes of the quality management system.

First, the quality manual must define and detail the 'scope of the quality management system'. This quality management system can be defined as: 'What does my practice do and how do they do it?' Just what is a quality management system? A *quality management system* is the management structure and management systems that are used to control and direct the practice with regard to quality.

> IMPLEMENTATION GUIDANCE NOTE: The scope of the quality management system should be clearly stated; for example whether it applies to the whole practice, a number of sections, or a single section. It should include the practice's structures, responsibilities and authorities, procedures, processes and resources needed to ensure that the health service product and/or service is of the desired quality, i.e. the quality management system should address all factors affecting the quality of the relevant service it provides.

Second, the quality manual shall include system level *procedures*. In lieu of actually incorporating system level procedures within the quality manual itself, the ISO 9001:2000 standard allows a reference to such system level procedures either in the quality manual or an external document referenced by the quality manual.

---

[10]*Quality Manual*: Document specifying the quality management system of an organization.

Third, the quality manual or system level procedures should include and define the interaction between the processes of the quality management system. Normally these process interactions are described in system level procedures or in *work instructions*. IVF centers typically refer to work instructions as protocols or 'how to' documents.

There are a number of reasons for having a quality manual. The most compelling reason is that it is a requirement for registration to ISO 9001.

Other reasons for having a quality manual are that it:

- Defines the practice's quality policy

- Documents the quality system

- Is a good management aid to defining responsibilities of employees

- Shows management commitment to quality

- Can be used for training purposes

- Is useful as a marketing tool for potential customers

- Provides continuity of the system as personnel change

- Provides a basis for carrying out audits.

Preparing the quality manual

Before writing the quality manual it is worthwhile to consider who are the end users of the manual. This is necessary as it may dictate both the format and contents of the Manual. If it is written for a registration/certification body then it will have to include the specific minimum requirements of the ISO 9001:2000 standard.

The quality manual may be written to satisfy a customer, if so their requirements will have to be addressed as well as the requirements of the ISO 9001:2000 standard.

An IVF center may wish to write the quality manual solely to satisfy the needs of its own internal practice and fulfill the requirements of its own quality system. Consideration should also be given to the readers of the manual in terms of the language they use and can understand.

There is no defined format for a quality manual. Style and format can be a matter of personal choice. The important thing is that the quality manual addresses the requirements of the quality system that is in operation. It is useful to follow a structured system with its stated requirements. If the fertility service provider is seeking registration to ISO 9001 then these requirements will have to be addressed in your quality manual (see Books for Developing Quality Manuals ISO 10013.)

It is often difficult to decide what to put into the quality manual and what to leave out. Depending on the size of the practice and the complexity of the operation it is usually better to have a separate procedures manual (see System Level Procedures). This will contain all the written procedures for the operation of the quality system. It could also contain work instructions, checklists and training details, or these may be made into separate manuals. Each procedure, work instruction, etc. will be given its own number and will be referenced from the quality manual. In this way the quality manual can be kept compact, neat and tidy.

Proprietary information

The IVF center may have proprietary information that it does not wish to divulge. This information should be kept separate from the quality manual. This is particularly important if the practice plans to show its quality manual to customers or competitors. Remember once the quality manual leaves the practice premises you have no control over where it will end up. In circumstances like this, it may be useful to have an uncontrolled version of the quality manual for information and marketing purposes.

Page format

Each page of the manual should have a simple title block and have the following basic information:

IVF center's logo here	QUALITY MANUAL 'abc' IVF center	QSM X.X.X Revision: Rev. Date:
		Approved by: ___ Approved Date: ___

Responsibility section

Identify what people or departments are responsible. Use titles rather than naming personnel.

Responsibility for the quality manual

It is a requirement of the ISO 9001 Quality System Standard that one person is designated as a Management Representative with responsibility and authority for ensuring that the requirements of the quality system and ISO 9001:2000 standard are implemented and maintained. This person is usually the Quality Manager or Risk Manager so it is natural that part of his/her responsibility would include writing, coordinating and distributing the quality manual.

In acting as coordinator for the quality manual, the designated representative must have the full cooperation of everyone in the practice who is involved in quality and process-related policies and procedures.

Above all the practice's management must accept the quality manual and this acceptance must be made known throughout the practice.

Data collection

It will be necessary to collect all the information relating to the quality system in order to write the manual. To do this it will be necessary to get as much information as possible from the various departments within the practice.

Talk to the managers in each department and explain what is the purpose of collecting the required information and ask for their help. Work with departmental managers in documenting and developing the manual in their area. Get the managers to write the details for their areas of responsibility.

Writing the quality manual

The manual should be written in straightforward simple language using the present tense. Sentences should be short and to the point. In an attempt to impress your readers you may be tempted to show off your vocabulary. Do not use complex, rarely used words. Highly technical terms should not be used unless they are properly defined and explained.

The quality manual should be as readable as possible. This means writing at the level of the language used by people reading the manual.

It is very important that the quality manual is a statement of the activities in operation in the practice at the time. It should not cover what has been done in the past or what might be done in the future but must cover the here and now. It must not detail activities that are not being carried out – do not attempt to embellish the manual to make it look good.

The quality manual must be a reflection of the quality system

The detailed contents of each manual will vary considerably depending on the nature of the service and operation of the particular practice. It will also depend on the level of control to be applied to the particular operation. A management system conforming to the requirements of ISO 9001 may run up to 30 pages or so.

Contents of the quality manual

The following examples of the contents of a quality manual are geared towards the requirements of ISO 9001:2000.

Table of contents/index

This is self-explanatory and should be compiled on completion of the manual. It is useful to have a clear logical classification system using a number or coding – if necessary the system should be explained.

Introduction

This will state that the purpose of the Manual is to describe the activities to be followed for the control of the quality of the product or service produced by the practice.

Quality policy statement

This can be a very simple statement of the practice's quality policy enshrining the practices commitment to provide services of the highest quality standard for its customers.

ISO 9001:2000 defines the quality policy as the 'overall intentions and direction of a practice related to quality as formally expressed by top management'. The quality policy forms one element of the Corporate Policy. The quality policy will be signed by individuals such as the Quality Manager, Medical Director and Administrator ensuring commitment to the publication and acceptance of the policies, activities and system laid out in the quality manual.

Revision sheet/amendment sheet

This is a sheet for recording any alterations or changes to the quality manual thus ensuring that each manual contains a complete record of all changes.

Distribution list

The distribution list is used to show the number of manuals in existence and the names of those who have numbered copies.

Procedures for up-dating manual

This contains specific instructions to each holder of the quality manual as to the procedure to be undertaken so that each copy of the quality manual is maintained up to date. Amendments should be reviewed and approved by the person responsible for the quality manual.

Purpose of the quality manual

This purpose statement describes the quality manual as a working document containing the practice's general practice, policies and activities for achieving and maintaining the quality of its delivery services. The purpose statement can also cover the fact that the quality manual is a source of reference for all matters dealing with quality and can be used by potential customers as a means of assessing the practice's quality system.

Definitions and terminology

It is necessary in the quality manual to give a definition of terms used in subsequent sections of the manual so that a clear and complete understanding of its contents is possible. This is particularly true when terms peculiar to the practice or particular industry are used. ISO 9001:2000 is a useful reference for such terms.

Practice data

Since the quality manual may be given to customers, this page gives general details about the practice:

- Name, parent practice if any

- Products produced and/or service provided

- Number of staff

- Location

Quality system requirements

The previous sections of the quality manual are of an introductory and general nature. Now we come to the body of the manual, the nuts and bolts of the system. These sections will, of necessity, be the longest in the manual. Its length and content will vary according to the size of the practice, methods of operation, the kind of quality program and the type of product or service.

CLAUSE 4.2.1c: QUALITY SYSTEM LEVEL PROCEDURES

The ISO 9001:2000 standard requires the creation and use of 'procedures'. IVF practices that are accredited by different accrediting bodies are not new to the concept of writing policies and procedures.

> IMPLEMENTATION GUIDANCE NOTE: The quality manual does not have to be a stand-alone document. It can be a part of a broader-based document covering all aspects of IVF center's activities. It also does not have to be called a 'quality manual'. It can be given whatever title is suitable for the center. In some practices the Leadership Section of the Joint Commission on Accreditation of Healthcare Organizations (JCAHO) or accreditation manual may be deemed the 'Quality Manual' while in others it may be called the 'Plan for the Provision of Care'.

Procedures within the ISO 9001:2000 scheme are different from those mandated by accrediting bodies. ISO 9001:2000 procedures are used to ensure that practice's processes and their interactions are defined. By documenting the way processes operate within the framework of the practice, improvement within those processes may take place as personnel discover new and improved ways of carrying out defined tasks. The term 'procedure'[11] causes some confusion when implementing an ISO 9001:2000 quality management system in practices.

Quality system procedures are documents that describe how the quality management system is applied to a specific product, service, project or contract. These documents may also be referred to as 'quality plans'. Additionally, quality system procedures specify the ways to carry out an activity or a process.

---

[11] *Procedure:* Specified ways to carry out an activity or process.

ISO 9001:2000 Clause 4.2.1 identifies several different require-ments when documented procedures must be created or established. As stated previously, there are six system level procedures identified in the ISO 9001:2000 standard where procedures are required to be docu-mented.

They are:

- **4.2.3** Control of documents

- **4.2.4** Control of quality records

- **8.2.2** Internal audit

- **8.3** Control of non-conformity

- **8.5.2** Corrective action

- **8.5.3** Preventive action

Additionally, procedures are required to be documented when such pro-cedures are needed by the IVF center to ensure effective planning, oper-ation and control of the service delivery processes.

The ISO 9001:2000 standard does not specify any specific format when creating the quality manual. The document format(s) are the practice's choice, but the scope of the documented management system will need to address each of the ISO 9001:2000 requirements. When drafting quality system documentation remember that, whatever the format, keep the documentation structure organized, complete, easy to understand and carefully identified. The ISO 9001:2000 standard avoids any specifics on how this should be accomplished.

IVF centers may ask, 'How much documentation do I need to gen-erate?' ISO 9001:2000 Clause 4.2.1 Note 2, states that the amount of your practice's documentation depends on several factors:

Factor 1   The size and type of activities that are a part of the practice

If the IVF practice is rather small with simple or redundant activities, the amount of documentation required may be minimal. If the practice is a very large, multifunctioned practice, then a large amount of docu-mentation may be necessary in order to apply effective control over its processes.

Factor 2   The complexity of the processes and their interactions

Complex processes will always require more detailed procedures. Simple processes may not require the same level of detail as those with greater complexity.

Factor 3   The competence of personnel

IVF practices whose processes and activities are not complex and where a high degree of employee competency, training and education exists may not require copious amounts of detailed procedures or instructions. Practices whose processes and activities are complex and where a high degree of competency, training and education does not exist may require a larger number of detailed procedures or instructions.

The nature and extent of the documentation should satisfy the customer, contractual, statutory and regulatory requirements as well as the needs and expectations of its customers and other interested parties. It is worth remembering that lengthy written procedures are rarely read thoroughly – if at all! Keep procedures simple and easy to understand.

Procedures describe the way a particular activity is to be carried out. They should describe:

How is an activity carried out?

Who is responsible for each aspect of the activity?

What records need to be collected and maintained?

When the activity should be carried out?

Why the activity is to be carried out?

When writing procedures, remember the golden rules of procedure writing:

- Decide *what* you want to say

- Decide *how* you are going to say it

- Use *simple*, clear language

- Keep in mind who will read and use it; this should determine your *style* of writing

The art of procedure writing lies in making it neither too long nor too short; it should be brief but complete. A procedure should contain sufficient information to allow a newcomer to the activity to carry it out without having to seek guidance from colleagues.

A general rule is that no procedure should be longer than 3–5 pages plus attachments. If your procedure is longer than this you may need to consider whether it should be more than one procedure, or one procedure plus supplementary work instruction(s).

It is recommended that your written procedures are presented in a standardized format. This has three advantages:

(1) It assists the person writing the procedure to identify *what* information needs to be included, and *where* it should be included;

(2) It helps the person reading the procedure to find the information he/she may need quickly and easily, rather than having to search through what may be several pages to find it;

(3) It gives an auditor confidence that you have a disciplined and structured approach to your documentation!

It does not matter which format you use, what is important is that it is standardized. The following example illustrates a standardized format that is an industry-wide 'best practice' format.

Procedure writing format

Purpose   Identify the purpose of the procedure in specific terms (aims).

Scope   Identify the scope of the procedure, i.e. where its boundaries lie. Any exclusions or limitations should also be stated.

References/related documents   Identify and list any standards or specifications that are referred to in the procedure. Additionally, list any work instructions that may need to be read with the procedure.

Definitions   In this section any positions that have specific responsibilities within the procedure should be identified. Any words or terms with special significance should also be defined here, e.g. abbreviations.

Procedure/method   This section should really be a statement of the way it is intended that this activity should be carried out. It will state in detail the actions necessary to achieve the aims defined in the purpose section of this format.

The text in the procedure should describe the sequence of actions (drawn up previously on the flow chart). It should aim to be brief but must include statements of:

- What information is necessary to perform the procedure and what will be the result from it being implemented

- The responsibilities and duties of people undertaking activities described in the procedure

- The method by which customer requirements are to be met

- The specific checks used to monitor the activities and the records necessary to demonstrate that the essential tasks of the procedure have been correctly undertaken

- 'What if' actions that may need to be taken and the way to deal with any non-conformances

- The supporting documentation generated and the records that have to be kept

It may also be necessary to say why it should be done in a particular way if there is a specific reason for using one method from a range of possible alternatives.

Records   This section should identify the records that are to be retained as evidence that the task has been completed and as an assurance of quality. It should also define their timescale for retention.

Attachments   Flow charts, illustrations, sample forms, tabulations, etc. may be included as attachments.

Quality plan

The product realization section of ISO 9001:2000 refers to a quality plan. ISO 9000 defines a quality plan as a 'document specifying which procedures and associated resources shall be applied by whom and when to a specific project, product, process or contract'.

The quality plan usually makes reference to the parts of the quality manual applicable to the specific case. A quality plan is generally one of the results of quality planning.

Work instructions

ISO 9001:2000 contains requirements that work instructions, when deemed necessary, should be available. This implies that such documents be written down. Work instructions are those documents that are defined by the IVF and may be necessary for carrying out detailed work activities. Work instructions provide information about *how* to perform activities and processes consistently. Work instructions may be documented in the form of protocols, books, 'how to' documents, workflows, flow charts, etc.

The only reference to work instructions found in the ISO 9001:2000 standard is in Clause 7.5.1. This clause merely states that when carrying out the service delivery processes, such processes must be carried out under controlled conditions. The standard goes on to state that, '…controlled conditions shall include, as applicable, (b) the availability of work instructions…' Clause 7.5.1 (b) DOES NOT require the creation of 'work instructions' but states that they will be used 'as applicable'.

CLAUSE 4.2.1e: RECORDS

ISO 9000 defines a record as a 'document stating results achieved or providing evidence of activities performed'. Some of the purposes of quality records include but are not limited to:

- Demonstration that requirements have been met

- Traceability to products or services that were rendered

- Facilitation of appropriate preventive and corrective actions

Clause 4.2.4 (see p.44) provides additional requirements and more detailed information for control of records.

CLAUSE 4.2.3: CONTROL OF DOCUMENTS

The IVF practice should establish and identify what documents and data it must maintain control over. Such controlled documents should suit the practice's method and scope of operation. Document control applies to documents and data in the form of hard copy or on electronic or other media. Documents used to define, direct and control activities that affect the quality management system should be controlled.

During a recent evaluation of a hospital that was readying itself to implement ISO 9001:2000 the writer noted that the *Consent Form* and the *Medicare Reimbursement* form signed by patients during admission were each a year old and both contained outdated information. A more recent version of the forms was found in the print shop. The forms found in use were dated January 2000; the new revisions of the form found in the print shop were dated, January 2001; the writers' evaluation took place in July of 2001. This means that admissions had been using the outdated forms for more than 6 months! What potential risk is the hospital exposed to as a result of this error? How many more forms used within the practice that were out of date may lead to patient safety concerns or other professional liability issues? Are there similar issues in your IVF center?

The purpose of document control is to ensure that the necessary, accurate and up-to-date documents are available to those who need them. This is especially important in somewhat complex practices such as IVF programs. Document control covers the creation, distribution and retention of internal documents and the receipt, distribution and retention of external documents that affect the quality management system and the quality of the practice's service programs and services.

The document control procedure must describe and address the following:

- Approval, review, updating and change of documents

- Identification of documents (i.e. issue number, revision status, issue date)

- Distribution

There can be some difficulty in deciding what is a document and what is a record. A simple rule is that a document can be revised, whereas a record cannot. For example, a quality manual can be revised and is covered by this Clause 4.2.3, while a patient's medical record cannot be revised. This is a record and is covered by Clause 4.2.4.

Examples of typical documents for which control should be considered include the following:

- The quality manual

- System level procedures, policies and procedures

- Protocols, books

- Work instructions

- List of approved subcontractors, including casual staff

- Statements of regulatory requirements

- Policies and reference to requirements or external manuals, such as health department or national standards. Schedule forms and treatment program information

- Computer software and manuals

- Catalogues and similar patient/client literature

The IVF center should develop a method for ensuring that the above types of documents are available to staff, with an indication of where they might be found. Only current versions of the management system documents should be available and a means of identifying and withdrawing superseded documents should be documented within the procedure.

The method of document control may vary according to the type of documents concerned. For example, critical procedures such as embryo transfer protocols, surgery and anesthesia procedures need a tightly controlled system, whereas a list of approved suppliers might be circulated against an approved distribution list.

The type of control and records used to control documentation may vary according to the type and criticality of the document. For example:

- For the quality manual, policies and procedures, protocols, books and instructions, a formal system of numbered documents, controlled issue and who holds and maintains documents might be considered

- A less rigid control might be considered for other material, which is distributed according to an approved distribution list

- External documents such as forms, manuals, regulations and standards from external bodies need to be kept up to date and may need to be registered or issued through a library (see Documents of External Origin)

The main point is that the IVF practice should adopt a document control system that suits its method and mode of operation.

Where the practice finds it necessary to change a document, the documentation control procedure should document and identify the change-control methodology and who is responsible for review and approval of changes.

Forms control

Every practice uses forms in the day-to-day operations of their management systems. Forms are used to document that specific requirements have been met. Forms must be controlled and their approval documented. Forms should not be confused with records. Blank forms are considered 'documents' and must be controlled. Forms should be carefully evaluated. Over time, forms tend to proliferate and become redundant or obsolete. During recent consulting projects for developing ISO 9001:2000 quality management systems, several hospitals reported decreasing the number of forms being used by as many as 1000.

Documents of external origin

Documents that are not included in the quality manual, but are listed as 'Referenced Documents' may include the following:

- Strategic plans such as the practice's mission statement or business plan, goals and objectives

- The rights and responsibilities of patients/customers

- Accredited programs or services

- References to professional and other external bodies

- References to safety and emergency procedures

- Professional books, handbooks, Joint Commission, etc. standards

- Government policies (federal, state or local area), regulations and administrative books

- Computer software programs

CLAUSE 4.2.4: CONTROL OF RECORDS

Health-care practices should control any records and documents that the practice is required to maintain to meet legal and statutory obligations, and other records generated as a result of service delivery process. These include patient records, admission and discharge records, drug registers and goods receipts, and so forth. During several consulting contracts involving a wide array of practices, it was noted that there were no documented procedures regarding the identification, indexing, filing and retention times of records. This leads the writer to the conclusion that this is a missing element within many practices. Like many hospitals, IVF practices are similarly complex and integrated.

In addition to these requirements, a number of clauses in the standard refer to specific requirements for record keeping. Most service practices will have an established system for maintaining records, and therefore should begin by reviewing existing procedures against the requirements of the standard, only adding or simplifying procedures where appropriate.

Establishment of the quality system should not result in unnecessary paperwork or duplication of records, and the first step in assessing this clause should be an evaluation of existing records and the effectiveness of existing record-keeping procedures.

Archiving and retrieval procedures, retention times, provisions for access to and methods of disposal for such records should be set down in procedures.

Where records are kept electronically, procedures may need to include systems such as archiving, maintenance of the software needed to access old records, backups and procedures for safe storage of electronic media such as computer disks.

The bottom line is – records must be identified, indexed, filed, stored and disposed of in accordance with documented procedures.

SUMMARY

In summary, an IVF center must document its management system, address each ISO 9001:2000 requirement and arrange information in an orderly manner. This leaves a lot of flexibility for building a quality management system in order to meet the needs of its business and the needs and expectations of customers. The structure of the documentation may be in any manner that works for the entire practice.

Chapter 4

ISO 9001:2000 Clause 5 – Management Responsibility

Leadership: IVF leaders establish unity of purpose, direction, and internal environment of the practice. Leadership creates the environment in which people can become fully involved in achieving the practice's objectives. Everything rises and falls on leadership!

CLAUSE 5.1: MANAGEMENT COMMITMENT

Executive management maintains the sole responsibility to define and document its responsibilities for quality and to ensure that the goals, objectives and commitment for and to quality are being met. The executive management must ensure that the quality system is implemented and effective in order to enhance customer/patient satisfaction and produce continual improvement throughout the practice.

Clause 5 – Management Responsibility

5.1 Management Commitment

TOP MANAGEMENT has to show their commitment to:

- Make everyone know how important it is to meet our customer needs
- Establish a quality system, including a quality policy, quality goals and quality planning
- Review the quality system to make sure it is working
- Make sure we have what we need to do our jobs

Practice priorities that relate to enhancing the service provided and improving patient outcomes are critical components in the delivery of services. Management must ensure that all services being provided are meeting the defined and documented quality policy, goals and objectives, which will bring about effective quality management and continual improvement.

CLAUSE 5.2: CUSTOMER FOCUS

Top management must demonstrate and ensure that customer requirements are being met with the aim of enhancing customer satisfaction. The IVF center must identify suitable methods to determine that patient/customer needs and expectations are being met in order to enhance customer satisfaction. This verification will most likely be identified during the implementation of Clause 7.2 Customer-related Processes as well as measuring of customer satisfaction in Clause 8.2.1 Customer Satisfaction. The practice must establish:

- That personnel have the necessary skills and expertise (see Clause 6.2.2 Competence, Awareness and Training) to determine what customer needs and expectations are

- That the practice has the capability of meeting the determined customer needs

Customer focus – who is the customer?

The ultimate goal of any continual improvement effort is to satisfy the needs of the customer to a higher degree. Thus, before formulating any continual improvement

Clause 5 – Management Responsibility

5.2 Customer Focus

TOP MANAGEMENT make sure that:
- We understand what our customers want and need
- Their wants and needs are made into requirements
- Customers requirements are understood and met

goals or strategic targets, the IVF practice must first assess who are their customers – just who are the customers that the practice supports? Focusing on customers can raise fundamental questions about the purpose and mission of the practice. When identifying customers the practice should ask the following questions from Dr W. Edwards Deming (Out of the Crisis. MIT Press, 2000) to assist in stimulating thinking about customers:

Who makes decisions about whether to purchase your service or product?

How do you distinguish between 'quality' as your customer perceives it and 'quality' as the practice's staff and leaders perceive it?

How does the quality of the product or service delivery, as the customer sees it, agree with the quality that the practice intends to provide?

- Do the practice's customers think that the product or service delivery lives up to their expectations?

- What does the IVF center know about the problems of customers in the use of the product or the service that was delivered?

- What tests are made to validate the product or service delivery processes?

- Does the IVF center depend on complaints from customers to learn what is wrong with the product or service?

- Are customers satisfied with the product or service delivery that is provided? If yes what is satisfactory about it? How is that known?

- Will the practice's customers of today be the customers a year hence? Two years hence?

Information concerning customers can be gathered from a large number of sources. As discussed in Chapter 1, the IVF center must identify customer requirements. In order to do this, the practice must identify who is the customer. Information concerning customers can be gathered from a number of sources. One method of identifying customer requirements is to gather a team of different department personnel and complete a 'customer affinity diagram'. Since most practices have many different customers, it is typical for them to separate customers into smaller subgroups, often referred to as segments. Most practices segment customers based on what products and/or services they use. Customer segmentation assists in defining the requirements of different groups. It also provides a basis for understanding similarities among customers. Additionally, it clarifies which customers can be impacted by improvement efforts focused on particular products or services delivered.

IMPLEMENTATION GUIDANCE NOTE: In many cases patient/customer needs (what they want) and expectations (what they expect to receive) are not the same. For example a patient may 'expect' a particular outcome for a medical condition. However, this expectation may be beyond the capability of current medical interventions and/or knowledge. Do not ignore this aspect. How has the practice communicated this to the patient/customer?

CLAUSE 5.3: QUALITY POLICY

The IVF center must have a documented quality policy (see Implementation Guidance below) that clearly reflects its mission, vision, goals and objectives, and takes account of the requirements and expectations of its patients and other customers. The quality policy must include some element of continual improvement.

Clause 5 – Management Responsibility

5.3 Quality Policy

TOP MANAGEMENT shall establish its quality policy and make sure that it:

- Is appropriate for the organization and its customers
- Includes commitment to meeting requirements and continual improvement
- Has quality objectives so they can be used and reviewed
- Is understood and used by all employees
- Is reviewed to make sure it still fits the organization

The practice should have established how it would communicate the quality policy to its staff. Methods for such communication should include: staff meetings, orientation sessions, workshops, public seminars, training sessions, e-mail, intranet sites, posters, bulletin boards, wallet-sized cards, etc. All personnel must understand their role in implementing the quality policy as well as meeting the practice's stated mission, values, goals and objectives. One important aspect of communicating the quality policy is ensuring that all staff members understand the practice's goals and objectives relating to the needs and expectations of patients/customers as well as the community at large. Patients/customers should be made aware of the practice's quality policy, values and objectives.

The quality policy needs to be reviewed periodically by management and should reflect changes in processes, activities and the changing needs and expectations of its patients/customers (Clause 5.6 Management Review).

IMPLEMENTATION GUIDANCE NOTE: The 'quality policy' may already exist as part of the fertility service provider's current strategic planning process or corporate mission/vision statements. This is not uncommon in the industry. Typically the provider will define, document and publish a mission statement or similar statement of vision, purpose or commitment. Practices sometimes choose to initiate a practice-wide 'mission or vision statement' independent of their quality system aspirations. Provided that there are measurable elements to such statements, and that these statements reflect the requirements in ISO 9001:2000, Element 5.3, then these statements may be used in lieu of the ISO term 'quality policy'.

CLAUSE 5.4: PLANNING

Planning within an ISO 9001:2000 management system includes such activities as planning and establishing quality objectives and then carrying out quality management system planning by top management.

Clause 5 – Management Responsibility

5.4   Planning

5.4.1 Quality Objectives

TOP MANAGEMENT shall ensure that quality objectives are established at relevant functions and levels. They must be measurable and include those objectives needed to meet customer requirements

Planning tools

There are many planning tools being used today by management. One of the most popular tools used today is Hoshin planning. Hoshin planning is driven through a practice-wide process where a vision is created and action is taken. The term 'Hoshin' is derived from a Japanese term, *hoshin kanri* meaning 'policy deployment'. The practice formulates a plan, transforms action plan inputs into measurable plan outputs or results and then conducts an internal audit (see Clause 8.2.2 Internal Audit) of the plan.

CLAUSE 5.4.1: QUALITY OBJECTIVES

In order to implement an effective quality policy top management needs to establish quality goals and objectives within the practice. These objectives may relate to both the quality management system and its improvement, as well as to those products and/or services that are provided by the provider.

Quality objectives need to be realistic and must have some measurable component attached to them. As the IVF center delivers and provides day-to-day care to patients/customers it achieves and carries out its objectives. The achievement of objectives is measured through the measuring and monitoring of delivery processes. As processes are measured and monitored, objectives are evaluated as to their effectiveness to meet requirements; objectives should be amended or new objectives developed based on the measuring and monitoring results.

IMPLEMENTATION GUIDANCE NOTE: The following table may be used when evaluating the practice's quality policy and objectives. Keep in mind that the quality policy and objectives should have been established to provide focus and direction to the practice.

Quality policy	Quality objectives
Defined: Overall intentions and direction of a practice related to quality as formally expressed by top management.	*Defined:* Something sought or aimed for, relating to quality.
Is the quality policy consistent with the overall policy of the practice?	Are objectives based on the practice's quality policy?
Does the policy provide a framework for establishing and setting quality objectives?	Are objectives specified for various functions and levels within the practice?
Does the policy provide a framework for reviewing quality objectives?	Are objectives consistent with the quality policy?
Does the quality policy identify the commitment of management to meet requirements?	Do objectives demonstrate a commitment to continual improvement?
Does the policy establish a commitment for continual improvement?	Is achievement of objectives measurable?
Is the policy communicated throughout the practice and is it understood?	Does achievement of objectives provide a positive impact on service delivery, operational effectiveness and financial performance?
Is the policy reviewed for continuing suitability?	Does achievement of objectives provide a positive impact on the satisfaction and confidence of patients/customers?

IMPLEMENTATION GUIDANCE NOTE: While evaluating the IVF center's 'Quality Goals and Objectives', top management shall ensure that the objectives created by the practice are S.M.A.R.T. objectives:

Specific — objectives must be Specific and relate to the quality policy.

Measurable — objectives must have some Measurable components.

Attainable — objectives that need to be Attained need to be within the practice's reach.

Reasonable — objectives must be Reasonable and contain logic.

Timely — objectives must have a defined Time frame.

It is common to find departmental goals and objectives defined in larger provider facilities. In these cases, each departmental manager and/or director provides yearly continuous quality improvement (CQI) plans that often include departmental objectives.

CLAUSE 5.4.2: QUALITY MANAGEMENT SYSTEM PLANNING

Once quality objectives have been established, the IVF practice must identify how it proposes to meet its quality objectives. The practice should include the development and documentation of a planning process or processes consistent with the practice's quality system and the way it operates. At some practices each departmental manager and/or director may be required to provide yearly continuous quality improvement (CQI) plans that often include departmental objectives.

The IVF center must be able to demonstrate that practice planning activities have been conducted and performed. Such

Clause 5 – Management Responsibility

5.4 Planning

5.4.2 Quality planning: activities and resources for quality, must be documented

- Plan processes, scope of ISO
- Plan quality resources needed to achieve desired results
- Plan continual improvement of the quality management system
- PLANNING SHALL ENSURE THAT change is conducted in a controlled manner and that the integrity of the quality management system is maintained during this change

planning activities establish the means by which the requirements for quality will be met. In lieu of detailed plans, quality system documentation such as procedures, policies and procedures, protocols, etc. may fully satisfy the quality management system planning requirements. Planning should also include how the quality and service delivery requirements for a particular service will be met, and how clinical inputs (diagnosis and interventions) and outcomes will be verified or evaluated. This may require planning from both a strategic and an operational level, as follows:

(1) *Strategic planning:* for example, may include planning a new scope of service (such as prenatal genetic diagnosis) that will be offered, identifying and allocating adequate resources to support the new service. Strategic planning may involve input from the community at large, customer feedback, changing demographics of the area such as an increasing or decreasing population, and other consumer groups.

(2) *Operational planning:* for example, may include the setting out in a planning document or other documented procedures the specific practices, resources and sequence of processes and activities relevant to the particular infertility service, project or contract.

Quality management system planning should also cover both clinical and non-clinical processes within the management system. The planning documents and records of planning must demonstrate and identify how objectives will be achieved.

> **IMPLEMENTATION GUIDANCE NOTE:** Documents or activities that demonstrate effective quality management system planning include: strategic business plans; quality objectives for a specific activity or system-wide activities; CQI plans and minutes from CQI meetings; meeting minutes from planning meetings; the design, delivery and evaluation of protocols, policies and procedures, and processes to ensure that practice is feasible and integrated within the system; design and development of nursing care plans; resources facilitating infrastructure procedures, tests, examinations or patient-outcome standards; establishing and documenting thresholds; patient charts and the documenting of patient assessments; measuring and monitoring of care plans at appropriate stages during the patient's stay, etc.

Planning output documents should be in a format that fits the needs of the IVF practice. Personnel need to be familiar with these documents. For standard clinical activities, planning may be achieved through the use of existing policies and procedures or by developing training programs. Management system plans can be as brief as a checklist or a workflow that may include reference to other parts of the management system. For new activities, services or processes the development of a specific planning document, procedure or manual may be necessary. The processes included in this document can then be adopted as standard policy or procedure, once the activity is firmly established. *Note* See also Clause 7.1 Planning of Product Realization.

CLAUSE 5.5: RESPONSIBILITY, AUTHORITY AND COMMUNICATION

CLAUSE 5.5.1: RESPONSIBILITY AND AUTHORITY

The infertility care provider shall identify and define what personnel are expected to do (responsibilities) and what they are allowed to do (authorities). This can be communicated by use of a practice chart. Functional areas of responsibility and authority within the practice can be shown on the practice chart. This chart can also show lines of communication (see Clause 5.5.3 Internal Communication). Practice charts can also specify accountability. Alternatively, responsibilities, authorities and accountabilities (and communication paths) may be described in the quality manual or other procedures.

CLAUSE 5.5.2: MANAGEMENT REPRESENTATIVE

The management representative is selected by top management to oversee the ISO 9001:2000 quality management system, to report on its effectiveness and to communicate the importance of meeting customer requirements (see Clause 5.5.3 Internal Communication). The management representative may work full-time in the area of quality, or can have other functions or responsibilities; the authority referred to in Clause 5.5.1 above applies when acting in the role of management representative. The ISO 9001:2000 standard requires that the appointed management representative be 'a member of management'. This appointment is very important, as the management representative must have the respect and equality amongst their peers to carry out the duties of implementing the management system. They should have a direct report to top management.

CLAUSE 5.5.3: INTERNAL COMMUNICATION

As with all practices, communication is the greatest weakness. In implementing an effective quality management system, an effective communication methodology must be implemented. The IVF center must maintain an internal communication system that enhances service delivery processes as well as the effectiveness of the quality management system. Electronic communication via Intranets, Internets and e-mail provides an effective and flexible approach. This form of communication allows for communication both upwards through the practice, as well as downwards. Other methods such as memoranda, postings on bulletin boards, staff meetings, either formal or informal methods, also have a place in this process.

Clause 5 – Management Responsibility

5.5 Responsibility, Authority and Communication

5.5.1 Responsibility and authority

5.5.2 Management representative

5.5.3 Internal communication

CLAUSE 5.6: MANAGEMENT REVIEW

ISO 9001:2000 requires top management to review the effectiveness of the quality management system at regular intervals. Records of management review must be maintained and must demonstrate any actions that were considered necessary regarding the quality management system, what action was undertaken and its effectiveness. Management review is conducted to evaluate the health and vitality of the documented management system at defined intervals.

The frequency and depth of management

Clause 5 – Management Responsibility

5.6 Management Review

5.6.1 General

Top management reviews the quality management system at planned intervals – to make sure that the system is suitable, adequate and effective. The need for change in the quality management system must be evaluated. Include review of quality policy and objectives

5.6.2 Review input to include:

- Audit results
- Customer feedback
- Process performance
- Status of corrective and preventative actions
- Follow-up from management reviews
- Changes that effect the quality system

reviews should be in line with the quality management system and the associated risk identified within each part of the practice.

Management review should include a review of the effectiveness of the quality management system as a whole at least once a year, with more frequent and detailed attention to critical areas and to areas where significant changes are planned or will be taking place.

Management review is an evaluation at the strategic level rather than the operational. It should, for example, include review of practice policies, practice priorities, success in the achievement of quality objectives, changes within the quality management system and allocation of capital and other resources.

CLAUSE 5.6.2: MANAGEMENT REVIEW INPUT

In many practices, committees frequently carry out reviews of the practice's operations. These reviews are **NOT** considered management review but information that may be needed during the management review. Findings and recommendations of such committee reviews may become an input into management review. In the same way the findings of internal audits should also be an input into the management review. Top management should ensure that it has not confused internal audits with management review (see Clause 8.2.2 Internal Audit). In addition to the items already mentioned, other activities that may be considered during management review include:

- Review of the quality management system's suitability and its effectiveness in achieving objectives for quality

- Progress towards the practice's strategic, operational, business and performance objectives

- Changes to legislation or statutory regulations, which may affect the practice's activities

- Analysis of data and trends in clinical indicators, thresholds and outcomes

- Customer feedback, including complaints, suggestions and reports

- External reviews by JCAHO, HCFA, State, CAP, CLIA, AOA, etc.

- Third-party audit reports, including internal quality audits (see Clause 8.2.2)

- Quality improvement, CQI reports, including reports from the management representative (see Clause 5.5.2 Management Representative)

- Non-conformities, corrective and preventive action reports (see Clauses 8.5.2 Corrective Action and 8.5.3 Preventive Action)

- Training and competency needs, and the practice's needs for competent, qualified personnel (see Clause 6.2.2 Competence, Awareness and Training)

- Changes to operational methodology

- Performance of suppliers (see Clause 7.4 Purchasing)

CLAUSE 5.6.3: MANAGEMENT REVIEW OUTPUT

The effect of any changes identified at the previous management review should be assessed. Additional action may be required if the changes do not achieve the desired effect. During the management review, the opportunity for justifiable improvement should be sought and implemented, resources permitting (see Clause 6 Resource Management).

Clause 5 – Management Responsibility

5.6 Management Review
5.6.3 Review output
- Include actions related to improvements in the processes/the quality management system
- Include improvements related to customer requirements
- Include actions related to resource needs
- Results of management reviews are recorded

In addition to the items already mentioned, outputs to management review should include decisions and actions related to:

- Improvement of the documented management system

- Improvement of its practice processes

- Improvement of the service delivery processes

- Improvement of customer satisfaction

- Resource needs

Records of management review

The management representative shall ensure that records of management review are maintained. The records could be minutes of a formal meeting held for the sole purpose of conducting management review or a report summarizing the key issues and actions to be implemented as a result of management review. A memo providing a summary of issues and actions to be taken may also be provided as a record of management review. Remember actions arising from management review must be followed up. The registrar will be looking for action follow-up during surveillance.

Chapter 5

ISO 9001:2000 Clause 6 – Resource Management

Involvement of people: a practice is comprised of people. A practice achieves maximum benefit when employees are fully involved, using their abilities to the practice's greatest advantage.

CLAUSE 6: RESOURCE MANAGEMENT

The skills, training, education and competence of all personnel providing care in an IVF center have a direct bearing on the quality and positive outcome of patient care. Both clinical and non-clinical personnel have a bearing on the patient/customer's expectations and perceptions of the care received. Therefore, the level of qualifications and training required for all personnel performing activities affecting quality needs to be identified.

Clause 6 – Resource Management

6.1 Provision of Resources

The organization shall determine and provide in a timely manner, the resources needed to establish and maintain the quality management system

Top management ensures that adequate resources are available. Resources include human resource management and the need to communicate to all staff an awareness of the practice's quality policy and objectives and an awareness of their roles in meeting your practice's values and objectives for patient care, both individually and as part of a team.

Records of personnel training and qualifications, and details of responsibility and authority specified in position or job descriptions can be developed to complement other quality documentation and records.

These records are normally part of human resource management records, and can form an important part of the quality management system. When creating documentation the practice should review the job or position description and compare it to the experience, qualifications, knowledge and skills of assigned staff. Hiring of staff could be considered under this clause, or Clause 7.4 Purchasing in the case of contract staff. Records of competency, training and education must be available (see Clause 4.2.4 Control of Records).

Training records should be available for activities such as:

- Safety and emergency procedures

- Compliance issues

- Skills and knowledge

- Communication skills

- Management skills/knowledge

- Technical or skill-related knowledge

- Quality management skills/knowledge

- Occupational health and workplace safety procedures

- Attendance at conferences, seminars and similar

- Opportunity for formal study

- Structured on-the-job training

CLAUSES 6.3 AND 6.4: INFRASTRUCTURE AND WORK ENVIRONMENT

These two clauses of the ISO 9001:2000 standard describe control of all the physical facilities that the IVF center needs to operate, including the working environment.

One important attribute of infrastructure is the maintenance of plant equipment. A preventive maintenance system needs to be identified and maintained. Many times there is little or no distinction within practices between preventive maintenance of equipment (Clause 6.3

Infrastructure) and calibration of equipment (Clause 7.6 Measuring and Monitoring Equipment).

During recent consulting projects in several hospitals the writers noted that the management personnel of biomedical facilities did not understand the difference between calibration of equipment and preventive maintenance of equipment. For example, in five hospitals evaluated, fetal monitors had not been 'calibrated' as required by the manufacturer's user manual.

Clause 6 – Resources Management

6.2   Human Resources
   6.2.1   General
   6.2.2   Competence, Awareness and Training
6.3   Infrastructure
6.4   Work Environment

This was particularly disturbing, as one hospital had settled a lawsuit regarding a fetal monitor that had failed. The fetal monitors in all hospitals evaluated were found to be logged within the practice's preventive maintenance system, but were **NOT** calibrated as per the manufacturer's user manual. In fact, biomedical personnel were completely unaware that the manufacturer's user manual addressed five pages of calibration requirements!

In several hospitals, the writers noted that numerous pieces of equipment were found to be in use that had entered the hospital's system by way of sales personnel who had 'loaned' the equipment on a trial basis. This equipment had by-passed the normal equipment entry process and was not in the preventive maintenance or calibration system. Calibration is discussed in detail in Clause 7.6

The IVF center must pay special attention to ensure that:

- Preventive maintenance of equipment is carried out and documented

- Electrical checks have been conducted on all electrical equipment in patient care areas

- Infection control procedures (Universal Precautions and Blood Borne Pathogens controls) are adhered to

- Air exchanges and temperatures in surgical suites are monitored

- Air filters are changed and maintained

- Emergency equipment is tested on a regular basis

✦ Surgical suite decontamination process is effective to prevent infection, etc.

Note: These activities are normally referred to by the Joint Commission on Accreditation of Practices as the 'Environment of Care'.

This chart may be used to define the training, competency and education requirements of clinical and medical staff.

IMPLEMENTATION GUIDANCE NOTE: Practices qualify physicians/clinical staff using a process known as Credentialing and Privileging.

Physician/clinical credentialing	Physician/clinical privileging
Defined: The process of verifying the credentials, license, education, training, experience, competence, health status, and judgment of any medical staff that may be granted clinical privileges.	*Defined:* Authorization granted by the hospital administration to provide specific patient care services in the practice within defined limits based on an individual practitioner's license, education, training, experience, competence, health status and judgment.

Methods of credentialing		Methods of clinical privileging	
Core privileges	Delineation of privileges	Core privileges	Delineation of privileges
The physician's credentials, license, education, training, experience, competence, health status and judgement are verified and, after approval, privileges are granted.	The physician's credentials, license, education, training, experience, competence, health status and judgment are verified by checking references and verifying that the professional has experience in the clinical procedures checked off in each block of the checklist.	Utilizing the hospital's defined Scope of Service a minimum core list of medical procedure groupings are created and listed. Privileges are granted based upon the general core categories on the list. Exceptions may be granted based on hospital needs and verification of credentials.	A standard list of common surgical procedures are are listed on a standard checklist. The physician indicating what procedures they are requesting to perform at the hospital checks off the appropriate blocks.

continued

continued

Verify:	Verify:	Verify:	Verify:
1) Core credentialing procedure.	1) Credentialing procedure.	1) Core privilege procedure.	1) Delineation of privilege procedure.
2) Check sample physician records.	2) Check sample physician records.	2) Check sample physician records.	2) Check sample physician records.
3) Verify that procedure is being followed.	3) Verify that procedure is being followed.	3) Verify that procedure is being followed.	3) Verify that procedure is being followed.
Ease of use:	**Ease of use:**	**Ease of use:**	**Ease of use:**
Less time-consuming	Time-consuming	Less time-consuming	Time-consuming

Chapter 6

ISO 9001:2000 Clause 7 – Product and Service Realization

Process approach: the IVF center's desire is to achieve more efficiency when related resources and activities are managed as a process.

CLAUSE 7.1: PLANNING OF SERVICE DELIVERY

ISO 9001:2000 Clause 5.4 Planning, discussed in Chapter 4, was focused on the higher-level strategic planning processes: the *who, what* and *why* of the IVF practice. Clause 7.1 focuses on the detailed operational level planning that identifies and defines *how, when* and *where* to deliver a service. Planning at the operational level should include functional or departmental objectives for each type of service that will be delivered. This level of planning should be consistent with the overall quality policy and objectives defined by top management.

In planning how delivery processes/services will be carried out, the practice must determine:

(1) Departmental or functional quality objectives and requirements for service delivery;

(2) The need to establish infertility care delivery processes and documents, and provide resources specific to the service delivery;

(3) The required verification, validation, monitoring, inspection and test activities specific to the service delivery process and the criteria for service acceptance;

(4)   The records needed to provide evidence that the delivery processes and resulting service meet requirements (see Clause 4.2.4 Control of Records).

CLAUSE 7.2: CUSTOMER-RELATED PROCESSES

CLAUSES 7.2.1 AND 7.2.2: REQUIREMENTS RELATING TO THE SERVICE DELIVERY

This clause of the standard primarily requires the practice to understand fully its customer's requirements prior to offering or agreeing to provide the service. Because of the different professionals making up an IVF center and the subsequent interface between numerous departments, service delivery requirements must be identified and documented at all levels of the practice.   The following implementation guidance note describes several clinical and non-clinical activities where customer requirements are determined and how they are documented. The term 'contract' is used in terms of agreements between the practice and its customers/patients.

IMPLEMENTATION GUIDANCE NOTE: Types of 'requirements' that may be identified include but are not limited to:

Clinical (Internal requirements)	Clinical/non-clinical (External requirements)
Informed consents	Nuclear medicine provider contracts
Anesthesia plans	Emergency Medical Service contracts
(Anesthesia counseling)	
Advanced directives	Food service contracts for other facilities
Patient advocate forms	Laundry service contracts to other facilities
Physicians orders and discharge orders	Lab service contracts
Consent for treatment	Blood banking
Patient financial responsibility agreements	Physician and other clinical staff contracts

As stated earlier, there can be a difference between what the patient/customer expects at the point of services rendered compared to what the practice is able to provide. Prior to the delivery of service, the practice must establish with the patient/customer exactly what services are to be provided and how rendered services will fulfill the customer's needs and meet or exceed their expectations. All services offered, such as pre-admission testing, social services, pharmacy services and other services, program information, costs and billing, testing, screening, treatment options, diagnosis and interventions and probable outcomes must be presented in a clear and concise picture to the patient/customer. All marketing literature should be consistent with the products and services offered by the IVF practice. Such materials should be current and up-to-date. (see Clause 4.2.3 Control of Documents).

In some cases, patients may enter the IVF facility alone and may lack the capacity to make decisions. In this case, the documents listed above may not be completed prior to admission or prior to the provision of care in the center. When next of kin is notified or the patient is able to make decisions, the above documents will be completed.

Clause 7 – Product Realization

7.1   Planning of the Realization Process

- Achieve consistent operation by establishing effective realization methods and practices
- Determine and implement criteria and methods to control processes and service delivery
- Verify that processes can achieve conformity to customer requirements

Physician orders may be provided and issued verbally. This is an acceptable method of receiving customer requirements provided there is documented evidence in the medical record and the processing of standing orders is described in applicable procedures or protocols. It is important that standing orders remain current and that changes made to the order indicate some level of control and acceptance. Additionally, a documented procedure should be established regarding the carrying out of standing orders.

In addition to knowing just who the customer is, the IVF center must also address what customers want and how to measure (see Clauses 8.23 and 8.2.4 Measuring and Monitoring) whether they are getting what they want.

Customers' needs and expectations are usually tapped through their perceptions and reactions to the use of current products or services. Customers are often concerned only with the requirements related to quality, cost and timeliness. Communication with patients/customers during the service delivery process is paramount in meeting customers' perceptions and in fully satisfying them.

CLAUSE 7.2.3: CUSTOMER COMMUNICATION

Depending on the particular IVF center, the practice may choose to provide some type of health information services to its patients/customers. This could take the form of a regular newsletter or information data sheets made available on a 'need-to-know' basis. Additionally, community activities sponsored by the IVF cen-

Clause 7 – Product Realization

7.2   Customer-related Processes
    7.2.1   Determination of customer requirements
    7.2.2   Review of product (service) requirements
    7.2.3   Customer communication

ter may be advertised via community mailings, public service announcements, newspaper advertisements, television advertising, social service departments, etc. For example, in the USA, the Joint Commission for Accreditation of Healthcare Organizations (JCAHO) requires the practice to establish communication channels for employees to identify delivery services that are unacceptable. In fact, some practices are required to have a grievance process in place. An effective ISO 9001:2000 management system will assist the practice in defining and carrying out a process to ensure that communication channels are open and working.

CLAUSE 7.3: DESIGN AND DEVELOPMENT

In some cases, design or development activities may be applicable, in others not. If design or development is NOT applicable, the practice must exclude this from their quality management system. Exclusions are normally documented in the quality manual stating the reasons why design or development activities are not conducted within the scope of service provided by the practice.

When design or development is applicable the following criteria shall be verified:

- Who is carrying out the work

- What the design or development activities are

- The stages in the design or development plan and the intermediate steps and activities

- The authorities and responsibilities for each stage or activity

- Design or development inputs

- Design or development outputs and validation

- Other participating departments, practices or support services

- Who is involved when the design or development plan changes

The above documentation does not need to be elaborate or extensive. In many cases, a simple flowchart may suffice. Where the planning interventions, diagnosis, thresholds, assumptions or circumstances change, the plan may have to be changed or modified. Such changes should be recorded and require authorization and approval from appropriate personnel.

Clause 7 – Product Realization

7.3 Design Control

7.3.1 Design and Development Planning
7.3.2 Design and Development Inputs
7.3.3 Design and Development Outputs
7.3.4 Design and Development Review
7.3.5 Design and Development Verification
7.3.6 Design and Development Validation
7.3.7 Design and Development Changes

All personnel involved in planning design activities should be suitably qualified or experienced to perform the work being undertaken.

IMPLEMENTATION GUIDANCE NOTE: The following is an example of a design or development activity in the practice setting.

Stage of design or development for a Nursing Plan of Care	Activity	Responsibility	Record
Design and development planning	Identify prognosis	Physician	Chart
Design and development inputs	Diagnosis	Physician and nurse	Chart/computer
Design and development outputs	Plan of care and interventions	Nursing staff	Chart/computer

continued

continued

Stage of design or development for a Nursing Plan of Care	Activity	Responsibility	Record
Design and development reviews	Review care plan interventions	Nursing staff	Chart/computer
Design and development verification	Verify effectiveness of interventions (output meets input)	Nursing staff	Chart/computer
Design and development validation	Validate efficacy of interventions	Nursing staff	Chart/computer
Final design and development validation	Provide discharge instructions	Physician, social services and/or nursing staff	Chart/computer then to medical records

For uncomplicated care, Nursing Care Plans may require only one care plan review at the completion of treatment. For very complicated services and care that require a high degree of complexity, several care plan reviews may be required as the patient responds to treatment and new information and patient assessment data become available.

Design or development verification (ISO 9001:2000 Clause 7.3.5) is the process of checking the results and outcomes of the plan in order to ensure that the Nursing Care Plan conforms to the identified interventions, i.e. measuring that the design stage output (interventions) is consistent with the design stage input (diagnosis) and that the patient's condition is either improving or not improving. Care plan design verification is a progressive operation that may be carried out over a number of shifts or days depending on the patient's response to treatment and the complexity of the care plan.

The IVF practice's design procedure should include details of the verification methodology to be adopted, including who is to carry out design verification and how it is to be performed and documented.

Design validation (ISO 9001:2000 Clause 7.3.6) is the process of confirming (by assessment, observation and examination) that the patient's expected outcomes meet the requirements.

The practice's design procedure should include details of how the Nursing Care Plan changes are identified, documented and reviewed.

The procedure should also establish who is authorized to review and approve changes.

CLAUSE 7.4.1: PURCHASING PROCESS

The practice should document a procedure for conducting its purchasing activities. In many settings, especially hospitals, it is not uncommon to purchase all or most of all supplies from one source of supply. A documented procedure should be established that defines the necessary purchasing controls.

Clause 7 – Product Realization

7.4 Purchasing
7.4.1 Purchasing Control
7.4.2 Purchasing Information
7.4.3 Verification of Purchased Product

CLAUSE 7.4.2: EVALUATION OF VENDORS AND SUBCONTRACTORS

The ISO 9001:2000 standard requires that the practice evaluates, selects and re-evaluates its vendors. The term 'vendor' is defined as a practice or individual that supplies or provides a product and/or service to the practice.

Evaluations of vendors and suppliers may use the following chart for guidance.

IMPLEMENTATION GUIDANCE NOTE: The practice may elect to evaluate its vendors in a number of different ways as follows.

Type of evaluation	Evaluation basis
Historical data	The basis for this selection is normally based on past experience with the supplier. Records indicate that the supplier has provided goods or services on a consistent and reliable basis.
On-site assessment	This selection method is based on the practice visiting the supplier location and conducting a formal evaluation of their ability to provide acceptable products or services. On-site assessments may be conducted for: • Treatment programs purchased from suppliers • Verification of vendor qualifications • Audit of suppliers or consultants • Commercial consultancy services, etc.

continued

continued

Type of evaluation	Evaluation basis
Third-party registration	This selection method is based on the supplier having a certified ISO 9001 quality management system by an accredited independent certification body (registrar). The supplier's certified system should cover the products or services the practice plans to purchase.
Reputation	This selection method is based on the supplier's reputation. References from other customers may serve as objective evidence of such a selection.
Desktop evaluation	This selection method is based on a questionnaire sent to the supplier asking them to self-evaluate their ability to provide acceptable products or services. The questionnaire is returned to the practice and evaluated for meeting defined criteria defined in the practice's documented procedure. If the supplier is acceptable they are then approved for use.
Provisional selection	This selection method is used when a new supplier is being considered on a trial basis over a specified period (say 3 months) or for a specific application. Acceptance as a permanent supplier would then be dependent on the results.

Methods other than those listed above in the implementation guidance notes could also be used. Whatever method or combination of methods is used to assess suppliers, documented procedures should formulate the basis of assessing vendors and potential vendors.

ISO 9001:2000 requires the practice to define the type and extent of control, which it will exercise over its vendors/subcontractors. For example, the control that the hospital has over physicians could be the peer review process or utilization review (UR) process. Studies are usually conducted at practices to track unusual, costly or repeated events (high-cost, high-volume, problem-prone, high-risk areas). By assessing such areas, the practice may verify that a process/system is implemented to demonstrate the capability and performance of subcontractors/vendors as well as to verify and establish the extent and control exercised by the vendors over their vendors/subcontractors.

CLAUSE 7.4.3: VERIFICATION OF PURCHASED PRODUCT

The IVF center's procedures should address receiving or incoming inspection and evaluation methods that are to be applied and what the acceptance criteria will be for incoming medical supplies and products. The purpose of receiving inspection is to ensure that the practice receives what it ordered. Additionally, such receiving activities can be used to evaluate the ongoing acceptability of vendors to meet the practice's requirements. Incoming inspection or evaluations of supplies and products could also include inspecting new equipment, evaluating new services that are supplied and materials to be used. In most practices receiving inspection usually consists of count, quantity and inspection for damage.

Measuring and monitoring (assessment and inspection) may also be applied to incoming patients with respect to the recognition of prior treatment and medical history: assessment of patients and development of treatment and care plans at admission; check of progress against the original interventions defined for each stage of the patient's care plan; and identification of special considerations or possible difficulties for a particular patient. These same considerations could also be addressed under Clause 7.2.2 Review of Requirements Related to the Service Delivery.

CLAUSES 7.5 AND 7.5.1: CONTROL OF PRODUCTION AND SERVICE PROVISION

This is the heart of the quality management system. The ISO 9001:2000 standard requires that the practice carry out its service delivery processes in a 'controlled manner'. What does the word 'control' imply? The ISO 9001:2000 standard throughout uses the term 'control'; for example, Control of Documents, Clause 4.2.3, Control of Records, Clause 4.2.4, Control of Non-conforming Products, Clause 8.2.3, etc. and all have requirements for controlling the defined processes.

Control implies that activities and processes used to carry out the service delivery process must be managed, overseen and organized in such a manner as to provide customer confidence of the practice's ability to satisfy stated or implied needs.

Methods that an IVF program may employ to ensure effective 'control' over its processes should include but should not be limited to:

➤ The availability of documentation or other reference information that the practice's personnel may require that describes the specifics of the service to be provided and/or delivered (i.e. PDRs, Care Plans, Radiographic Position Guides, etc.)

- Ensuring that protocols, work instructions and other documents defining the methodology and processes are available for use by personnel

- Ensuring that adequate equipment needed to carry out the service delivery processes are available and in good working condition

- Ensuring that measuring and monitoring equipment is in a calibrated state and ready for use

Processes must be evaluated and defined. The IVF center should carefully study all delivery processes, both clinical and non-clinical during the management system development phase of the implementation process. The processes include, but are not limited to:

- Office-based services (non-surgical)

- Emergency services (ambulatory)

- Emergency services (hospital admission required)

- Pre-admission through discharge (non-surgical)

- Surgical services

- Pathology and laboratory

- Embryology and andrology services

- Specialized services such as embryo biopsy

- Anesthesia services

- Maintenance and facilities management department

- Social work services

- Radiology/imaging services

Compliance with reference standards/codes is required by the ISO 9001:2000 standard. Due to the nature and number of regulatory requirements within the industry, it would be impossible to list these requirements here. A list of these standards/codes should be available and under control at the facility. Such requirements are typically regulated by the country and local authorities.

Continual improvement of the management system focuses on linking customer requirements (Clause 7.2.1 Determination of Customer Requirements) with both product/service *characteristics*[12] and quality characteristics. ISO 9001:2000 Clause 7.5.1b states that in order to control service delivery effectively, information that describes the service delivery characteristics must be available. In other words, how do I know that I am doing a good job? What are the characteristics or requirements that are available to ensure that the job was carried out according to plan?

ISO 9001:2000 Clause 4.1a and b states that the practice should identify the processes needed for the quality management system and their application throughout the practice as well as determining the sequence and interactions of these processes. When consulting, our practice utilizes flow charting of work processes to meet these requirements.

What are flow charts? Flow charts are graphical representations of the way a work process is carried out. It describes the path that a process follows from start to finish.

What is a process? A process as described earlier is a 'set of interrelated or interactive activities that transforms inputs into outputs'. Inputs from one process may be the outputs of another process. For example, a patient presents at admission for an ultrasound examination procedure. The

Clause 7 – Product Realization

7.5   Production and Service Operations
   7.5.1   Control of Operations and Service Delivery
   7.5.2   Identification and Traceability
   7.5.3   Customer Property
   7.5.4   Preservation of Product
   7.5.5   Validation of Processes

patient presents to the physician, and typically the test is ordered in the computer by the doctor for the admission personnel. The physician's order (output document) becomes the input document that begins the ultrasound procedure. The resulting output of the physician is the order which is also the input to the ultrasound examination.

The ISO 9001:2000 standard focuses on process management, continual improvement and enhancing customer satisfaction. Effective process management requires that core processes be identified and improved upon. Continual improvement focuses on processes. A

---

[12]*Characteristic:* distinguishing feature of a process or service

Basic Flow Charting

process must be understood if improvement is to take place. In the flow chart:

The *parallelogram* is the symbol that is used to depict the process inputs, i.e. *Ultrasound receives the physician's order.*

The *rectangle* depicts the process steps that will be carried out, i.e. *Ultrasound reviews the physician's order.*

The *diamond* describes when a decision must be made, i.e. *Can the physician's requirements be met?*

The *circle* indicates that there is a connection between this process and another process or another document, i.e. *Pre-testing may have been required.*

The *rectangle* with *curved bottom* depicts that some document or record is referenced. This symbol may or may not be used, i.e. *Refer to the policy and procedure for admitting the patient and the handling of physician's orders.*

The *rounded rectangle* completes the process and creates the output that becomes the input for the next process, i.e. *Patient admitted for ultrasound and patient record created.*

This is a basic example of flow charting techniques and symbols. As can be seen from the examples that follow, flow charts may be basic and very linear in nature or may take several more complex paths. Remember that a flow chart is a map and that a map provides directions from point A to point B. Examples of flow charts can be found in Appendix 4.

CLAUSE 7.5.2: VALIDATION OF PROCESSES

Processes that may require 'validation' include but are not limited to, laboratory protocols, sterilization, laboratory procedures such as sperm preparation and fertilization procedures, etc. The process employed must be qualified and carried out by qualified personnel following approved procedures. Since providers would generally be using appropriately qualified personnel and established procedures for their treatment regimes, compliance with the requirements of this clause should not present any difficulties.

CLAUSE 7.5.3: IDENTIFICATION AND TRACEABILITY

The IVF practice should be able to identify and trace patients, relevant information, correspondence, data, material and other items throughout the facility. Additionally, patients/customers shall be identified to ensure that appropriate treatment is given. For example, patient/customer identification numbers can be used to provide traceability to relevant records. Banding of patients is yet another method. Bar coding and using adhesive labels may be used to provide identification and traceability of blood tests, blood products and associated documentation such as test records.

Data, records (such as assessment notes in medical records) may also be required as identification and traceability requirements. Clause 4.2.4 Control of Records covers the retention and storage of data and records,

IMPLEMENTATION GUIDANCE NOTE: Examples of where identification and traceability apply in the practice include but are not limited to.

Nursing	Pharmacy	Laboratory
Patient identification (bands, patient ID numbers)	Patient identification (bands, patient ID numbers)	Patient identification (bands, patient ID numbers)
Medical charts (patient IDs)	Doses of medications	Laboratory results, bar codes
Treatment schedules	Controlled substances	Quality control/test protocols
Central sterile (ID of biological indicators)	Unit dose carts, and medication sheets	Treatment schedules

while Clause 7.5.5 Preservation of Product would be appropriate for materials.

CLAUSE 7.5.4: CUSTOMER PROPERTY

The term 'customer' may be defined as follows: the recipient of the service provided by the IVF center (e.g. non-staff doctors, patients, family members of patients, community at large, etc.); in contractual situations, the customer may also be referred to as the 'patient'; the customer may be the ultimate consumer, user, beneficiary, or purchaser of the practice; a customer may be both internal and external.

Customer property is defined as follows: items that require a special degree of handling, care and maintenance; personal belongings that the customer provides to the facility, which will be returned to the customer or the customer's designee at some agreed-upon time or at the completion of the service provided; examples of customer property are patient-supplied medications, donated eggs or sperm, donated embryos, etc.

The practice must ensure that all customer property is identified, verified, stored and maintained as required, using the definitions above as a guideline when identifying 'customer property'. The practice should take note that there is a relationship between 'Clause 7.4 customer property' and 'Clause 7.5 preservation of product'.

CLAUSE 7.5.5: PRESERVATION OF PRODUCT

Preservation of product within the sector will be applied very broadly. Due to the nature of the types of services provided, preservation of product covers a wide range of areas and services; (e.g. mobility of patients from department to department, transportation of patients from the procedure room to their ride home, medical records, ultrasound reports, and test results supplied or provided by the patient. Handling and preserving includes tests, test specimen and test reports for evaluation, newborns, medications, medication/materials with limited shelf-life, etc.)

Preservation includes the protection of customer's (patient's) possessions that the IVF center is responsible for or comes into contact with.

Limited shelf-life is an important aspect to consider when documenting the ISO 9001:2000 preservation of product requirement. A common example of this may be out-of-date medication. Limited shelf-life controls must be in place in the pharmacy and laboratory, to ensure that the items in use are not expired.

CLAUSE 7.5.6: MEASUREMENT AND MONITORING DEVICES

Health-care facilities maintain a plethora of measuring and monitoring devices. A procedure must be established to control the calibration process. Examples of where calibration may apply could include:

- Diagnostic equipment

- Test equipment

- Software (where the need for calibration has been identified)

- Measuring devices used in a research project

- Measuring devices used with incubators, embryo freezers and other equipment where pressure or temperature is critical

This clause of the standard sets out requirements for control of measurements which the practice is required to address to ensure that measuring and monitoring equipment as well as equipment which could affect outcomes, or is used to verify outcomes, is appropriate for use, is properly maintained and properly calibrated before use.

Calibration that is traceable to some national standard (see Clause 7.6a) is not essential in all cases. For example, although anesthetic gauges need to be identified and calibrated, the gauges on individual gas bottles connected via a manifold would only need a periodic check, provided that they are used to indicate an adequate supply (volume) of gas, and not to measure pressure accurately during administration of gases to the patient. For some equipment, such as electronic equipment used to provide a go–no-go indication, periodic safety and function checks and maintenance may be adequate in lieu of calibration. Equipment where there is a low risk of variation may not require calibration at all (for example, thermometers, manometers and cuffs may be exempt due to the low risk of variation relative to the application).

In addition to equipment, requirements for control may need to include the accuracy of software applications (e.g. where specified in an assessment, and likely to affect patient outcomes).

Also, routine servicing and maintenance of measuring and test equipment would normally not satisfy the requirements for calibration (see discussion in Clause 6.3 Infrastructure of this book). In developing the procedures for calibration of measuring and monitoring devices, the IVF center should include a requirement

Clause 7 – Product Realization

7.6 Controlling and Measuring and Monitoring Devices

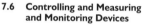

- Identify equipment
- Choose correct equipment for the job
- Calibration is traceable to a national standard

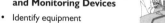

that if a measuring or monitoring device is found to be outside of the calibration range, the consequences of possible inaccuracies of prior measurements need to be considered. If necessary, remedial action (such as recall or retesting) may need to be taken.

Chapter 7

ISO 9001:2000 Clause 8 – Measurement, Analysis and Improvement

Factual approach to decision-making: the IVF center must base decisions on the logical or intuitive analysis of data and information.

CLAUSE 8.2.1: CUSTOMER SATISFACTION

In conjunction with the practice-wide strategic and departmental planning, the carrying out of the service delivery controls and process implementation plans, the practice shall measure and monitor strategies, goals, targets and objectives

Clause 8 – Measurement, Analysis & Improvement

8.1 Planning
8.2 Measurement and Monitoring
  8.2.1 Customer satisfaction
  8.2.2 Internal audit
  8.2.3 Measuring and monitoring of processes
  8.2.4 Measuring and monitoring of product

to ensure effective operation and control and to ensure that customers' requirements and perceptions are being met. The industry is one where statistically based evidence is commonly used (see Clause 8.4 Analysis of Data).

As an infertility care practice there may be some issues or problems in reconciling the differences between what a patient/customer may perceive as an expectation and what the fertility care provider can actually deliver by way of treatment or a care program. For example, a patient may *expect* that you can provide a *'cure'* for a particular cause of infertility, whereas the known state of the medical knowledge on the particular cause of infertility may not be treatable. This may well apply where the best possible service was delivered but the expectations were not achieved, thereby producing a negative perception of the outcome. Handling such situations requires professionals to possess and demonstrate excellent communication skills.

CLAUSE 8.2.2: INTERNAL AUDIT

Internal audits of the quality management system processes shall be carried out at defined intervals. Additionally, internal audits shall cover the ISO 9001:2000 requirements. Process audits (assessments) of the internal management system are a relatively new concept in the community. Many practices focus on 'chart audits' and 'compliance audits'. Neither one of these types of audits are conducted to evaluate the system processes of the entire practice's management system and structure but are narrowly focused in specific areas using specific audit criteria.

Are there ISO standards for conducting internal audits of management systems? Yes. ISO10011:1, 2, and 3 are audit standards published by the International Practice for Standardization that define specific requirements for the qualification of audit personnel, define good audit methodology and provide direction to the practice on how to manage the audit process. The ISO 10011:1, 2 and 3 document is in the revision stage and will be renumbered as ISO 19011:2001. ISO (10011) 19011 provides guidance on the fundamentals of auditing, the management of audit programs, the conduct of quality (as well as environmental) management system audits and the qualifications for management system auditors. It is applicable to all practices and the carrying out of both internal and external audits.

What is an 'internal quality audit' of the management system? ISO 9000:2000 defines an internal Quality Audit as, 'a *systematic, independent* and documented process for obtaining *audit evidence* and evaluating it objectively to determine the extent to which *audit criteria* are fulfilled'.

Elaborating on the definition, a *systematic* audit is one that is well planned and proceeds through the different stages of the audit life cycle. It is *independent* in the sense that, as per ISO 9001:2000, 'auditors shall not audit their own work'.

Audit evidence in ISO 9000:2000 is defined as 'records, statements of fact or other information which are relevant to the audit criteria and verifiable. *Note*: audit evidence can be qualitative or quantitative'.

Audit criteria in ISO 9000:2000 is defined as a 'set of policies, procedures or requirements used as a reference'. In relation to procedures it is important to view them in a broader context than just documented procedures.

Purpose of auditing

There are several reasons for performing an audit of the quality system. The major reasons are as follows:

- To permit the listing of the audited practice's quality system in a register

- Quality system standards, such as ISO 9001 require that an internal audit be performed

- To meet regulatory requirements such as the Food and Drug Administration (FDA) good manufacturing practices in the USA

- To assist with the selection of vendors

- To determine the conformity or non-conformity of the quality system elements with specified requirements, such as ISO 9001:2000

- Management requires assurance that the quality system can deliver quality products and services which meet agreed customer requirements and customer expectations

- To determine the effectiveness of the implemented quality system in meeting specified quality objectives

- To provide the auditor with an opportunity to improve the quality system

The last reason given above is becoming increasingly important for practices whose quality systems are maturing. At this stage compliance may not be the major issue, but continuous improvement. The audit in essence, is used as a proactive tool to identify opportunities for improvement throughout the system.

A number of clauses in ISO 9001 are closely associated with improvement (see Clause 8.4 below). These include:

- Internal Audits (Clause 8.2.2)

- Continual Improvement (Clause 8.5.1)

- Corrective Action (Clause 8.5.2)

- Preventive Action (Clause 8.5.3)

- Management Review (Clause 5.6)

Auditor's responsibilities

Auditors are responsible for:

- Complying with the applicable audit requirements

- Communicating and clarifying audit requirements

- Planning and carrying out assigned responsibilities effectively and efficiently

- Documenting the observations

- Reporting the audit results

- Verifying the effectiveness of corrective actions taken as a result of the audit

- Retaining and safeguarding documents pertaining to the audit, and submitting such documents as required

- Ensuring such documents remain confidential

- Treating privileged information with discretion

Human aspects of conducting internal audits

Initial attempts to implement quality system audits meet resistance of varying degrees in most practices. There is natural resistance to any change, but people especially do not like change forced upon them. The greater the extent to which the change is being done *to* rather than *by* them, the greater the resistance to the change.

In the case of implementing an internal auditing activity, the cultural change that people will experience is both intrusive and critical – not only will their work areas be invaded, but also their work efforts will be critiqued. People who have been performing their jobs perhaps for years without scrutiny will now have their behavior subjected to the review of others.

For this reason, the auditing function should not be justified based on some external need for its existence. It does not comfort the fearful staff and other professionals to know that the auditing system is required by standards such as ISO 9001:2000. They really do not care!

The reason that ISO 9001:2000 requires internal auditing is because it has intrinsic value. Staff and other professionals will be more receptive to auditing, if they know that its purpose is to find the cause(s) of job-related problems so that those problems may be eliminated and hopefully cause their job to be easier. This is a cultural issue: if the practice is introducing auditing into the workplace, the audit manager or the management representative become the change agents. The auditing function will operate smoothly if it is accepted as a valuable improvement tool. Therefore, much of the work in setting up an internal auditing process in the practice is to gain acceptance for its value.

To gain acceptance, the audit manager or management representative must educate the work force. Education can be handled through newsletters, memos, electronic mail, department meetings, and other available means. It is essential that the work force get the message about auditing, such as:

- What an audit is?

- How it is conducted?

- Why it is done?

- What the benefits are to the practice?

- What the benefits are to the auditee (staff and other professionals)?

- Why it should not create fear?

One last point should be stressed. One tactic that some practices have used when implementing an internal audit system is first to 'tell them' and then 'show them'. First, everyone is informed about how auditing is a benefit to people in their workspace. Second, pilot audits are conducted. The results are reported along with whatever problems were found and subsequent corrective actions (opportunities for improvement) are identified. When people see that the audit in practice works to their benefit the way they were told it would, they will begin to overcome their fear. However, if the practice is going to make the audit process work, auditors and potential auditors must be carefully selected and instructed. Ideally, auditors should be good at putting people at ease and remain focused on issues that will really help a department to improve. You do not want auditors who are arrogant or nitpickers.

Management must also be prepared if the audit is going to work. Quality system auditing, like other 'quality'-related functions, should be described to management in terms of how it helps the practice to achieve its business and strategic goals, targets and objectives. If auditing is perceived to be something apart from the business of the practice, it will not be afforded much attention. If it is understood to be a tool to help uncover and remove problems that prevent the practice from operating effectively, economically and efficiently, then it will be valued. Once management understands this, they will be open to using the tool properly.

If the individual contributors in the practice are to accept the value of the auditing process, your management must first accept it.

Managers do not want to be judged by the number of problems found in their areas – especially if they became successful by covering up problems. If they think they will be judged in this manner, they may shift the 'blame' for problems to individual employees, thus, doing exactly what the audit manager or management representative told staff would not be done. Management must be convinced that auditing is a tool they can benefit from, not a weapon to be used against them or by them.

The same tactics that work for individual contributors work for managers. Teach them how the tool works and then using some pilot audits, show them how it works. As managers, they receive the output (non-conformity and corrective action requests) of the auditing function – they are the clients of the audit. The audit report that contains the list of opportunities for improvement goes to them. They are responsible for corrective action.

After obtaining management commitment, the next step is to define the audit infrastructure, describe the audit process, and write a detailed audit procedure so that audit consistency can be achieved. The audit procedure details responsibilities and activities of audit management, audit coordinator, audit team leader, audit team, auditee and management. The procedure thoroughly defines the audit process from planning and execution of the audit to reporting results, to documentation of the audit and follow-up of corrective action, to close-out of the audit and to record retention. The procedure is all-inclusive and leaves no requirement unstated.

Another important feature included in the procedure is the definition for an avenue of escalation for issues that cannot be resolved at the manager level. These issues might include delaying tactics by the auditee in scheduling an audit, disputed audit findings that cannot be resolved by the parties involved, or lack of response from the auditee in submitting a corrective action plan. Having a defined escalation process in place can remove the emotions involved in cases of disagreement or dispute.

CLAUSES 8.2.3 AND 8.2.4: MEASURING AND MONITORING OF PROCESSES AND PRODUCTS

The IVF program needs to establish appropriate assessments, tests or verification (checking) to be performed at the various stages of the delivery process. The assessments, tests or verification should be consistent with the operations and should be defined in appropriate procedures.

In many cases the procedures will cover the process and its assessments, tests or verification requirements, i.e. Clauses 7.5, 8.2.3 and 8.2.4. For example, assessment of patient/customer treatment plans could be addressed under Clause 7.5, or under this clause.

These two clauses cover the monitoring and measuring of processes and also of service delivery. In many instances the same technique will apply to both. For example, measuring how successful a treatment regime has been will, of necessity, measure the outcome with respect to the patient/customer's status. Monitoring and measuring could apply to:

- Assessment and evaluation of patient/customer outcomes

- Monitoring of treatment programs, such as a rehabilitation program

- Monitoring of administration systems

- Ensuring that equipment is functioning correctly

- Checking the continuing suitability of equipment and facilities

- Monitoring the use of consumable items, such as theater sets or perishables in catering departments

CLAUSE 8.3: CONTROL OF NON-CONFORMITY

In practices a 'non-conformity' is often known as a variance, occurrence or incident and is reported as such. Some examples of non-conformities in the facility (which could be due to lack of resources, e.g. facilities or equipment) are as follows:

Clause 8 – Measurement, Analysis & Improvement

8.3   **Control and Non-conformity**
8.4   **Analysis of Data**
8.5   **Improvement**
   8.5.1   Planning for continual improvement
   8.5.2   Corrective action
   8.5.3   Preventive action

- Inability to admit patients to treatments due to waiting lists

- Inadequate or inappropriate materials and services

- Equipment that is not functioning correctly or is out of service or out of calibration

- Out-of-date supplies, medication or drugs, which have not been disposed of properly

- Failure to meet legislative or regulatory requirements (such as State Health Department, HCFA, occupational health and safety regulations)

- Failure to meet procedures, standards or practice guidelines

- Deficiencies in the quality management system or procedures

- Patient injury

An example of when a non-conformity becomes reportable is as follows. If a laboratory technician finds a mislabeled sperm sample, but discovers and rectifies the error before the sample is used clinically, and the error is corrected by the technicians, this does not constitute a non-conformance. However, if the laboratory director discovers the error during a routine check, then this becomes a non-conformance that must be reported and corrective action must be taken to ensure that laboratory or pharmacy processes used are effective or need improvement.

CLAUSE 8.4: ANALYSIS OF DATA

Health-care practices such as IVF centers collect reams of clinical data. Few data are collected for the non-clinical areas. Support services are critical to the ongoing effectiveness of delivery processes and data need to be analyzed and evaluated. The IVF practice must collect information and data and manage it in a way that supports the practice's strategic and operational plans and objectives. The practice's information management system should be reviewed and maintained to meet the changing demands of the practice and external requirements such as demands for reports by accreditation or governing bodies. Areas where analysis (including statistical technique) might apply could include:

- Patient/customer satisfaction analysis

- Preventive action

- Collection and analysis of process information

Patient/customer data and clinical information should be analyzed to provide comparative analysis of outcomes, occurrences, incidents and variances, and to provide information that can become the basis for continual quality improvement (CQI). Where data are used to compare performance and evaluate outcomes, it is important that the procedures for collecting, reporting and exchanging information are compatible and based on sound statistical methods.

CLAUSE 8.5.1: CONTINUAL IMPROVEMENT

The IVF center needs to have a plan on how the quality management system can be improved. This improvement is known as 'continual improvement'. This term is not unfamiliar to practices. The five keys to continual improvement of an ISO 9001:2000 quality management system are depicted in the following graphic. When implementing an ISO 9001:2000 management system, the measuring and monitoring of both processes and service delivery must ensure that effective controls have been applied to the process and to ensure that service is being delivered in accordance with planned arrangements.

| Measuring and Monitoring | Internal Audit | Corrective Action | Preventive Action | Management Review | Continual Improvement |

CLAUSES 8.5.2 AND 8.5.3: CORRECTIVE AND PREVENTIVE ACTION

Both corrective and preventive actions are steps in a quality improvement cycle. The need for corrective action is generally initiated by the occurrence of a non-conformity, patient/customer complaint or similar event. Corrective action is taken to ensure that the cause of a problem is identified and action taken to prevent recurrence of the problem.

Preventive action is concerned with analyzing the system using the available data and information to identify causes of potential problems and thus eliminating possible causes of non-conformity or patient/customer complaints.

Procedures should be in place for both corrective and preventive action, with responsibilities and authorities defined. Patient/customer data and clinical indicators should be collected and used to monitor performance and to evaluate the outcomes of patient/customer care and the management of the service delivery process (see Clause 8.4).

The practice should establish a procedure to ensure constant and consistent review of:

- Adverse events and outcomes relating to patient/customer care

- Non-conformities, variances, occurrences and incidents

- Complaints from patients/customers and other third parties

- Deficiencies and areas for improvement identified by audits

- Internal reports, including suggestions

The above should be monitored by top management as key elements of an integrated system of incident, variances, occurrences and non-conformity reporting and continual quality improvement, which should be used to identify casual and contributing factors, and thus enable corrective and preventive actions to be taken.

The practice providing IVF services should also identify the cause of any problems arising from:

- Any failure of the quality management system

- Complaints from suppliers

- Unsatisfactory procedures

Irrespective of how the need for corrective action is identified, the practice should ensure that appropriate action is initiated and corrective action taken. Top management should ensure that the changes resulting from corrective action are followed up to make sure that they are effective.

Comparison between ISO 9001:2000 and MBNQA

ISO 9001:2000 vs. MBNQA

ISO 9001:2000	Malcolm Baldrige National Quality Award (MBNQA)
1. American National Standard containing minimum requirements for establishing a quality management system.	1. Comprehensive set of guideline criteria drafted around winning an award.
2. Criteria based on a process approach to management, continual improvement both clinical and financial as well as enhancing customer satisfaction.	2. Criteria based on winning an award. Practice makes a formal, detailed and highly documented application.
3. Third-party certification body is selected by the practice to perform a verification audit. ISO 9000 is not award based. Application process only seeks minimum information about the practice. Documentation is submitted for evaluation after which a site visit is ALWAYS conducted.	3. After application has been made and submitted, the application and documentation MAY trigger a site visit by a group of examiners. Site visit examiners sift through the practice verifying on site what the practice had written in their application.
4. The practice's focus: The implementation of an effective quality management system.	4. The practice's focus: Winning an award.
5. Late 1980s first ISO 9000 registered companies.	5. Late 1980s Xerox first winner.
6. Work is focused on documenting processes, internal audit of processes, continual improvement, improved leadership, data, etc.	6. Work is focused on the documentation required for winning the award rather than the underlying activity that the documentation is to represent.

continued

continued

ISO 9001:2000	Malcolm Baldrige National Quality Award (MBNQA)
7. Through the certification bodies ongoing annual surveillance assessments and the practice's measuring and monitoring of activities, processes and internal system audits, improvement is measured yearly by the external body. An ISO certified system IS THE WAY A PRACTICE CONDUCTS ITS BUSINESS. No need to return to the 'way it used to be'.	7. The concept of winning an award, while strongly compatible with the American love of a winner, leaves many practices with the belief that quality is a destination to arrive at; once there, practices can go back to how they had traditionally run their business.
8. While ISO 9000 certified practices have also filed bankruptcy, they do not obtain the same press that a Baldrige winner does. ISO is a system of processes certified and reassessed yearly by a third party.	8. Several winners of the MBNQA have turned out to be questionable at best. Wallace Company, Inc. filed bankruptcy protection from the same government who a year before had awarded them the Baldrige Award recognizing them as a great company.
9. *Summary*: Excellent exercise and process for bringing a practice together to enhance customer satisfaction, improve processes, solidify and to achieve a common practice-wide goal.	9. *Summary*: Excellent exercise and process for bringing a practice together to win the highest prize achievable within quality circles and to achieve a common practice-wide goal.
Short-term impact: Brings people together for a common goal. Personnel intimately involved with the process have great resumes and become targets for competing practices to steal away. Implementing the ISO 9001:2000 standard causes improvement in practice performance and process management.	*Short-term impact*: Provides the practice with national publicity. Winning the award creates a national perception that the practice has 'achieved' world-class quality. The award is an excellent marketing tool to use against competitors. Personnel intimately involved with the process have great resumes and become targets for competing practices to steal away. Implementing the MBNQA criteria causes improvement in practice performance and process management.

continued

continued

ISO 9001:2000	Malcolm Baldrige National Quality Award (MBNQA)
Long-term impact: Creates a continual and ongoing effort at improving processes never to return back to the way it used to be. After certification, there is ongoing third-party validation that the practice continues to meet and exceed the high standards that it was certified to. There is a requirement after initial certification to continue to comply with ones own requirements and to update the 'processes and systems' through annual surveillance from an accredited third party.	*Long-term impact*: A slow progression back to the way it used to be. After the award is won, there is no ongoing validation that the practice continues to meet the high standards that it won the award with. There is no requirement after winning the award to continue to comply with ones own requirements and to update the 'processes and systems' based on any new MBNQA criteria.
10. *Bottom line:* • Improved customer focus • More effective leadership • More involvement of people • Improved process management approach • Effective systems approach to management • Creates a system of continual improvement • Creates a system where decisions are made using factual data • Creates a mutually beneficial supplier relationship	10. *Bottom line:* As with any competition that was ever won, the participants and winners get old, worn out and tired. Most retire with the tale of what they accomplished during their career as a competitor. What they did accomplish is long forgotten by the public as new winners take their place and break their records. MBNQA brings about continual improvement over the short term but it is not a sustainable management system process as there is no requirements or systems in place for validating the practice's ongoing compliance with its own documented processes and the changing MBNQA criteria.

ISO 9001 Principles:	1. Customer focus	2. Leadership	3. Involvement of people	4. Process approach (management)	5. System approach to management	6. Continual improvement	7. Factual approach to decision-making	8. Mutually beneficial supplier relationship
MBNQA Criteria								
1. *Leadership*								
1.1 Organizational		❂ ❂						
1.2 Public responsibility & citizenship		–						
2. *Strategic planning*				–	–	–	❂	
2.1 Strategy development		–		–	–	–	–	
2.2 Strategy deployment		–		–	–	–	–	–
3. *Focus on patients, other customers and markets*	❂			–	–	–	❂	❂
3.1 Patient/customer & health-care market knowledge	–			–	–	–		
3.2 Patient/customer satisfaction & relationships				–	–	❂		
4. *Information & analysis*							❂	
4.1 Information of organizational performance		–				–	–	
4.2 Analysis of org. performance		–				–	–	

❂ ISO requirements are consistent with MBNQA criteria

❂ ❂ General areas of weakness in most health-care settings. Areas are required by both ISO 9000 and MBNQA

– ISO 9001 requirements *are* not completely consistent with MBNQA criteria but have some relationship

continued

ISO 9001 Principles:	1. Customer focus	2. Leadership	3. Involvement of people	4. Process approach (management)	5. System approach to management	6. Continual improvement	7. Factual approach to decision-making	8. Mutually beneficial supplier relationship
MBNQA Criteria								
5. Staff focus	✪		✪					
5.1 Work systems			–					
5.2 Staff education, training and development			✪					
5.3 Staff well-being and satisfaction			–					
6. Process management	✪			✪	✪	✪	✪	✪
6.1 Health-care service process	✪			✪	✪	✪	✪	
6.2 Support processes				✪	✪	✪	✪	
6.3 Supplier and partnering process								✪
7. Org. performance results	✪					✪		
7.1 Patient/customer focused results	–					✪		
7.2 Financial & market results	–							
7.3 Staff and work system results	–		– Staff ✪Work system results			–/✪		
7.4 Supplier and partner results						✪		✪
7.5 Organizational effectiveness results						✪		

✪ ✪ ISO requirements are consistent with MBNQA criteria

✪ ✪ General areas of weakness in most health-care settings. Areas are required by both ISO 9000 and MBNQA

– ISO 9001 requirements *are not* completely consistent with MBNQA criteria but have some relationship

ISO 9000:2000 Self-Assessment Instrument

INTRODUCTION

ISO 9001:2000 is an International Standard that defines requirements to assist practices in building a system for managing the quality of care provided at their facility.

The standard gives requirements for a quality management system that must be met. Your application of the standards should reflect the mission and values of your practice. Beginning with a succinct quality policy statement and set objectives, all facets of the quality management system focus on these goals and drive it to reality.

This is a system of documented procedures that are useful and up to date, indexed for ready accessibility.

What is important to your practice?

- YOU decide

- YOU voice a vision

- YOU make it happen...

with a quality management system to make quality dreams reality and keep them that way!

SCORING THE SELF-ASSESSMENT INSTRUMENT

Perspective

Take the perspective of people who do the daily work within the practice, rather than what management wants or leadership says. In other words, be as objective as possible about the current reality of your current systems and processes.

Scoring

Respond to each statement with a percentage of readiness corresponding to one of the following phrases that best describes how well your practice performs with respect to that statement.

Documentation

For statements related to *documentation* (prefixed by a 'D' on the score sheets), use these phrases:

20% – There has been discussion about the need for documentation. Alternatively, do not know.

40% – Rough drafts or outdated versions exist but are not used.

60% – Documentation exists, but it is superficial or is seen as insufficient or not useful.

80% – Documentation exists and is generally useful, but it is not always kept up to date.

100% – Relevant documentation is available, complete, useful and up to date.

Implementation

For statements related to *implementation* (prefixed by an 'I' on the score sheets), use these phrases:

20% – There has been discussion about the need for this. Alternatively, do not know.

40% – Applies to limited parts of the practice.

60% – Widespread awareness, but not done on a consistent basis across the practice.

80% – Consistently done in major parts of the practice, done sporadically in other parts.

100% – The norm for all major parts of the practice.

For the purpose of this tool, the ISO 9001:2000 standard has been broken into five parts entitled *Quality Management System, Management Responsibility, Resource Management, Production and Service Delivery* and *Measurement, Analysis and Improvement.* At the end of the five sections you will find score sheets for these sections. The score sheets are self-explanatory. The last page of the tool is a final scoring sheet. Tally up the results from the section score sheets and place them in the appropriate column of the final score sheet. Divide the total number by 5 and you will have your practice's percentage of readiness in obtaining ISO 9001:2000 certification.

Note: In some cases, not all of the questions will apply to your practice. If this is the case, simply add the number of scores that you did answer in a specific section and divide that number by the total number of questions answered. We hope that you find this tool useful as you consider adding ISO 9001 to your current management system in order to bring about continual quality improvement.

ISO 9001:2000 Clause 4 – Quality Management System

	Documentation					Implementation				
QMS1. A quality management system has been established, documented, implemented, maintained,and continually improved?	❑ 20	❑ 40	❑ 60	❑ 80	❑ 100					
QMS2. The quality management system includes: a.) identification of the processes needed for the quality management system? b.) determination of the sequence and interaction of these processes? c.) determined criteria and methods required ensuring the effective operation and control of these processes? d.) the availability of information necessary to support the operation and monitoring of these processes? e.) methods to measure monitor and analyze these processes? f.) implemented action necessary to achieve planned results and continual improvement?	❑ 20	❑ 40	❑ 60	❑ 80	❑ 100					
QMS3. Processes that are outsourced that affect product or service conformity are identified and documented?	❑ 20	❑ 40	❑ 60	❑ 80	❑ 100					
QMS4. The quality management system documentation includes written procedures and records required ensuring effective operation and control of its processes?	❑ 20	❑ 40	❑ 60	❑ 80	❑ 100					
QMS5. The extent of the quality management system documentation is appropriate to: a.) size and type of the organization? b.) complexity and interaction of the processes? c.) competence of personnel?	❑ 20	❑ 40	❑ 60	❑ 80	❑ 100					
QMS6. Responsibilities and authorities for all personnel are clearly understood and effective						❑ 20	❑ 40	❑ 60	❑ 80	❑ 100
QMS7. Responsibilities and authorities for all personnel are documented	❑ 20	❑ 40	❑ 60	❑ 80	❑ 100					
QMS8. A quality manual has been established which includes: a.) scope of quality system, including details and justifications for exclusions? b.) procedures or references to procedures? c.) sequence and interaction of QMS processes or reference to them?	❑ 20	❑ 40	❑ 60	❑ 80	❑ 100					
QMS9. Documents and their distribution required for the quality management system are controlled?						❑ 20	❑ 40	❑ 60	❑ 80	❑ 100
QMS10. There Is a documented procedure for: a.) the approval of documents for adequacy prior to issue? b.) the review, updating as necessary and re-approval of documents? c.) the identification of the current revision status of documents? d.) ensuring that relevant versions of applicable documents are available at points of use? e.) for ensuring that documents remain legible, readily identifiable and retrievable? f.) ensuring that documents of external origin are identified and their distribution is controlled? g.) preventing the unintended use of obsolete documents, and to apply suitable identification to them if they are retained for any purpose?	❑ 20	❑ 40	❑ 60	❑ 80	❑ 100					
QMS11. Are quality records for resources and system planning available?	❑ 20	❑ 40	❑ 60	❑ 80	❑ 100					
QMS12. Do these records provide evidence of conformance to requirements and of effective operation of the quality management system? Do the records determine what corrective and/or preventive action is necessary?	❑ 20	❑ 40	❑ 60	❑ 80	❑ 100					

ISO 9001:2000 Clause 5 – Management Responsibility

	Documentation					Implementation				
	20	40	60	80	100	20	40	60	80	100
MR1. Top management has demonstrated a commitment to the development and improvement of the quality management system by: a.) communicating to the organization the importance of meeting customer as well as regulatory & legal requirements? b.) establishing the quality policy? c.) ensuring that quality objectives are established? d.) conducting management reviews? e.) ensuring the availability of resources?						☐	☐	☐	☐	☐
MR2. Top management has ensured that customer requirements are determined and fulfilled with the aim of achieving customer satisfaction?						☐	☐	☐	☐	☐
MR3. Top management has ensured that the quality policy: a.) is appropriate to the purpose of the organization? b.) includes a commitment to meeting requirements and to continual improvement? c.) provides a framework for establishing and reviewing quality objectives? d.) is communicated and understood within the organization? e.) is reviewed for continuing suitability?						☐	☐	☐	☐	☐
MR4. Quality objectives have been established at relevant functions and levels within the organization?	☐	☐	☐	☐	☐					
MR5. Quality objectives are measurable and consistent with the quality policy?						☐	☐	☐	☐	☐
MR6. Quality objectives including those needed to meet requirements for product/service are defined?	☐	☐	☐	☐	☐					
MR7. Top management has ensured that: a.) processes of the quality management system are carried out in order to meet the requirements? b.) the output of quality planning is documented? c.) changes are conducted in a controlled manner to ensure that the integrity of the management system is maintained when changes occur? d.) how and what method is used when planning changes that may affect the quality management system?						☐	☐	☐	☐	☐
MR8. The functions and their interrelations within the organization, including responsibilities and authorities are defined and communicated?	☐	☐	☐	☐	☐					
MR9. Communication channels have been established within the organization relating to management system effectiveness?						☐	☐	☐	☐	☐
MR10. Top management reviews the quality management system, at planned intervals, to ensure its continuing suitability, adequacy, and effectiveness?						☐	☐	☐	☐	☐
MR11. This review evaluates the need for changes to the quality management system, including the quality policy and quality objectives?						☐	☐	☐	☐	☐
MR12. Opportunities for improvement and changes needed within the quality system are evaluated and documented?	☐	☐	☐	☐	☐					

continued

ISO 9001:2000 Clause 5 – Management Responsibility *(continued)*

	Documentation	Implementation
MR13. Inputs to management review include current performance improvement opportunities related to the following: a.) results of audits? b.) customer feedback? c.) process performance and product conformance? d.) status of preventive and corrective actions? e.) follow-up actions from earlier management reviews? f.) planned changes that could affect the quality management system? g.) recommendations for improvement?	❏ ❏ ❏ ❏ ❏ 20 40 60 80 100	
MR14. Outputs to management review include current performance and improvement opportunities related to the following: a.) improvement of the effectiveness of the QMS and its processes? b.) improvement of product or service related to customer requirements? c.) resource needs?		❏ ❏ ❏ ❏ ❏ 20 40 60 80 100

ISO 9001:2000 Clause 6 – Resource Management

	Documentation	Implementation
RM1. Resources needed to implement and improve the quality management system processes has been provided?	❏ ❏ ❏ ❏ ❏ 20 40 60 80 100	
RM2. Adequate resources are available to implement and maintain the management system and to continually improve its effectiveness?		❏ ❏ ❏ ❏ ❏ 20 40 60 80 100
RM3. Resources are available to ensure that customer satisfaction is enhanced?		❏ ❏ ❏ ❏ ❏ 20 40 60 80 100
RM4. Responsibilities and authorities of all personnel is defined and available?	❏ ❏ ❏ ❏ ❏ 20 40 60 80 100	
RM5. Personnel assigned responsibilities in the quality management systems are qualified and deemed competent based on skills, experience, and education & training requirements?		❏ ❏ ❏ ❏ ❏ 20 40 60 80 100
RM6. The organization has: a.) determined the necessary? b.) competency for personnel? c.) provided training to satisfy competency needs? d.) evaluated the effectiveness of actions taken? e.) ensured that its personnel are aware of their part in the QMS? f.)maintained appropriate records of education, training,skills, and experience?		❏ ❏ ❏ ❏ ❏ 20 40 60 80 100
RM7. The infrastructure of the organization is such that: a.) buildings, workspace, and associated utilities are determined, provided, and maintained? b.) process equipment, hardware, and software are determined, provided, and maintained? c.) supporting services such as transportation or communication are determined, provided, and maintained?		❏ ❏ ❏ ❏ ❏ 20 40 60 80 100
RM8. The organization has identified and managed the human and physical factors of the work environment needed to achieve conformity of product/service?		❏ ❏ ❏ ❏ ❏ 20 40 60 80 100

ISO 9001:2000 Clause 7 – Product/Service Delivery Realization

	Documentation	Implementation
PSR1. Planning of the product/service delivery processes is consistent with the other requirements of the organization's quality management system?		❏ ❏ ❏ ❏ ❏ 20 40 60 80 100
PSR2. Realization processes documented in a form suitable for the organization's method of service delivery and/or operation?	❏ ❏ ❏ ❏ ❏ 20 40 60 80 100	
PSR3. In planning product realization, the organization has determined: a.) the quality objectives and requirements for the product/service? b.) the need to establish processes and documents, and provide resources specific to the product/service? c.) the verification, validation, monitoring, inspection, test activities, and the criteria for product/service acceptability? d.) the records that are necessary to provide evidence of conformity of the processes and resulting product/service fulfill customer requirements?	❏ ❏ ❏ ❏ ❏ 20 40 60 80 100	
PSR4. The organization has determined customer requirements including: a.) product/service delivery requirements specified by the customer? b.) product/service delivery requirements not specified by the customer but necessary for intended or specified use? c.) obligations related to product, including regulatory and legal requirements? d.) additional requirements determined by the organization?	❏ ❏ ❏ ❏ ❏ 20 40 60 80 100	
PSR5. The organization reviews identified customer requirements along with any additional requirements determined by the organization.		❏ ❏ ❏ ❏ ❏ 20 40 60 80 100
PSR6. Is this review conducted prior to the commitment to supply a product to the customer?		❏ ❏ ❏ ❏ ❏ 20 40 60 80 100
PSR7. The review ensures that: a.) product/service delivery requirements are defined? b.) the customer provides no documented statement of requirement, the customer requirements are confirmed before acceptance? c.) contract or order requirements differing from those previously expressed are resolved? d.) the organization has the ability to meet defined requirements?		❏ ❏ ❏ ❏ ❏ 20 40 60 80 100
PSR8. The results of the review, actions, and subsequent follow-up actions recorded (see ISO Element 4.2.4)?	❏ ❏ ❏ ❏ ❏ 20 40 60 80 100	
PSR9. Where product/service requirements are changed, the organization ensures that relevant documentation is amended?	❏ ❏ ❏ ❏ ❏ 20 40 60 80 100	
PSR10. Verbal orders are handled, addressed, and documented?		❏ ❏ ❏ ❏ ❏ 20 40 60 80 100

continued

ISO 9001:2000 Clause 7 – Product/Service Delivery Realization *(continued)*

	Documentation	Implementation
PSR11. The organization ensures that relevant personnel are made aware of any changed requirement?		❑ 20 ❑ 40 ❑ 60 ❑ 80 ❑ 100
PSR12. Customer requirements are reviewed against orders before services are provided?		❑ 20 ❑ 40 ❑ 60 ❑ 80 ❑ 100
PSR13. The results of the review of requirements and any follow-up actions are recorded?	❑ 20 ❑ 40 ❑ 60 ❑ 80 ❑ 100	
PSR14. The organization has identified and implemented arrangements for communication with customers relating to: a.) product /service delivery information? b.) enquiries, contracts, or order handling, including amendments? c.) customer feedback, including customer complaints?	❑ 20 ❑ 40 ❑ 60 ❑ 80 ❑ 100	
PSR15. The results of the review of agreements and any follow-up actions are recorded?	❑ 20 ❑ 40 ❑ 60 ❑ 80 ❑ 100	
PSR16. Service delivery design and development planning methodology described in the design procedure?	❑ 20 ❑ 40 ❑ 60 ❑ 80 ❑ 100	
PSR17. The service delivery design and development stages planned and organized?		❑ 20 ❑ 40 ❑ 60 ❑ 80 ❑ 100
PSR18. Responsible personnel review, verify and validate each service delivery design and development stage?		❑ 20 ❑ 40 ❑ 60 ❑ 80 ❑ 100
PSR19. The interfaces between different groups involved in service delivery design are identified and managed?		❑ 20 ❑ 40 ❑ 60 ❑ 80 ❑ 100
PSR20. Service delivery design and development inputs relating to product/service delivery requirements are defined and documented?	❑ 20 ❑ 40 ❑ 60 ❑ 80 ❑ 100	
PSR21. Results of service delivery design plan verification activities are kept on file and readily accessible.	❑ 20 ❑ 40 ❑ 60 ❑ 80 ❑ 100	
PSR22. The outputs of the service delivery design and/or development processes are documented in a manner that enables verification against the service delivery design and/or development inputs?	❑ 20 ❑ 40 ❑ 60 ❑ 80 ❑ 100	
PSR23. Service delivery design and/or development output must: a.) meet the service delivery design and/or development input requirements? b.) provide appropriate information for production and service delivery operations? c.) contain or reference product/service delivery acceptance criteria? d.) define the characteristics of the product/service that are essential to safety and proper use?		❑ 20 ❑ 40 ❑ 60 ❑ 80 ❑ 100
PSR24. Service delivery design and/or development output documents are approved prior to release?	❑ 20 ❑ 40 ❑ 60 ❑ 80 ❑ 100	

continued

ISO 9001:2000 Clause 7 – Product/Service Delivery Realization *(continued)*

	Documentation	Implementation
PSR25. Records of service delivery design outputs is maintained and easily accessible?	❏20 ❏40 ❏60 ❏80 ❏100	
PSR26. Systematic reviews of service delivery design and/or development is conducted at suitable stages?		❏20 ❏40 ❏60 ❏80 ❏100
PSR27. These reviews: a.) evaluate the ability to fulfill requirements? b.) identify problems and propose follow-up actions?		❏20 ❏40 ❏60 ❏80 ❏100
PSR28. Participants in such reviews include representatives of functions concerned with the service delivery design and/or development stage(s) being reviewed?		❏20 ❏40 ❏60 ❏80 ❏100
PSR29. The results of the reviews and subsequent follow-up actions are recorded?	❏20 ❏40 ❏60 ❏80 ❏100	
PSR30. Records of service delivery design reviews maintained?	❏20 ❏40 ❏60 ❏80 ❏100	
PSR31. Service delivery design and/or development verification is performed at defined time periods to ensure the service delivery output meets the designand/or development inputs?		❏20 ❏40 ❏60 ❏80 ❏100
PSR32. The results of verification and subsequent follow-up actions are recorded?	❏20 ❏40 ❏60 ❏80 ❏100	
PSR33. Service delivery design and/or development validation is performed to confirm that resulting product or service delivery is capable of meeting the requirements for the intended use?		❏20 ❏40 ❏60 ❏80 ❏100
PSR34. Wherever applicable validation is completed prior to the delivery or implementation of the product?		❏20 ❏40 ❏60 ❏80 ❏100
PSR35. When full validation is impractical prior to delivery or implementation, partial validation is performed to the extent applicable?		❏20 ❏40 ❏60 ❏80 ❏100
PSR36. Are the results of the validation and subsequent follow-up actions recorded?	❏20 ❏40 ❏60 ❏80 ❏100	
PSR37. Service delivery/product design and/or development changes identified, documented, and controlled?		❏20 ❏40 ❏60 ❏80 ❏100
PSR38. Does this process include evaluation of the effect of the changes on service delivery/constituent parts or delivered products?		❏20 ❏40 ❏60 ❏80 ❏100
PSR39. Changes are verified and validated, as appropriate, and approved before implementation?	❏20 ❏40 ❏60 ❏80 ❏100	
PSR40. The organization controls its purchasing processes to ensure that purchased product conforms to specified requirements?		❏20 ❏40 ❏60 ❏80 ❏100

continued

ISO 9001:2000 Clause 7 – Product/Service Delivery Realization *(continued)*

	Documentation					Implementation				
	20	40	60	80	100	20	40	60	80	100
PSR41. The type and extent of control over vendors/suppliers is dependent upon the effect of the product or service delivered or produced?						❑	❑	❑	❑	❑
PSR42. The criteria for selection and periodic evaluation of vendors/suppliers is defined?	❑	❑	❑	❑	❑					
PSR43. The results of evaluations of vendors/suppliers and subsequent follow-up actions are recorded?	❑	❑	❑	❑	❑					
PSR44. Purchasing documents contain information describing the product to be purchased?						❑	❑	❑	❑	❑
PSR45. These documents include where appropriate: a.) requirements for approval or qualification of product, procedures, processes, equipment, and personnel? b.) quality management system requirements?						❑	❑	❑	❑	❑
PSR46. The adequacy of specified requirements contained in the purchasing documents is reviewed prior to document (POs, quotations, etc.) release?						❑	❑	❑	❑	❑
PSR47. When purchasing good/services, the purchaser provides vendors/suppliers with precise details of the order to ensure item/services are purchased correctly in the first place?						❑	❑	❑	❑	❑
PSR48. Activities necessary for the verification of purchased product has been identified and implemented?						❑	❑	❑	❑	❑
PSR49. The organization controls service operations through: a.) the availability of information that specifies the product characteristics? b.) the availability of work instructions? c.) the use of suitable equipment for production and service operations? d.) the availability of measuring and monitoring devices? e.) the implementation of monitoring activities? f.) the implementation of defined processes for release, delivery, and applicable post-delivery activities?	❑	❑	❑	❑	❑					
PSR50. The organization validates any production and service delivery processes where the resulting output cannot be verified by subsequent measurement or monitoring?	❑	❑	❑	❑	❑					
PSR51. Processes requiring validation include deficiencies that may become apparent only after the product is in use or the service has been delivered?	❑	❑	❑	❑	❑					
PSR52. Process validation demonstrates the ability of such processes to achieve planned results?	❑	❑	❑	❑	❑					
PSR53. Defined arrangements for validation include as applicable: a.) qualification of the process? b.) qualification of equipment and personnel? c.) use of defined methodologies and procedures? d.) requirements for records? e.) revalidation?						❑	❑	❑	❑	❑

continued

ISO 9001:2000 Clause 7 – Product/Service Delivery Realization *(continued)*

	Documentation	Implementation
PSR54. Products and/or service delivery is identified by suitable means throughout production and service delivery process where appropriate?		☐ ☐ ☐ ☐ ☐ 20 40 60 80 100
PSR55. Products are identified by suitable means throughout production and service operations where appropriate?		☐ ☐ ☐ ☐ ☐ 20 40 60 80 100
PSR56. The status of product with respect to measurement and monitoring requirements is clearly identified?		☐ ☐ ☐ ☐ ☐ 20 40 60 80 100
PSR57. Where traceability is a requirement, is the unique identification of product controlled and recorded?	☐ ☐ ☐ ☐ ☐ 20 40 60 80 100	
PSR58. The organization exercises care with customer property while it is under the control of or being used by the organization?		☐ ☐ ☐ ☐ ☐ 20 40 60 80 100
PSR59. Customer property is: a.) identified? b.) verified? c.) protected? d.) maintained? e.) if any customer property is lost, damaged, or otherwise found to be unsuitable for use is it recorded and reported to the customer?		☐ ☐ ☐ ☐ ☐ 20 40 60 80 100
PSR60. Products are preserved to ensure conformity with customer requirements and are maintained during internal processing and delivery to the intended destination? This includes the identification, handling, packaging, storage, and protection?	☐ ☐ ☐ ☐ ☐ 20 40 60 80 100	
PSR61. The organization identifies the measurements to be made and the measuring and monitoring devices required to assure conformity of product to specified requirements?		☐ ☐ ☐ ☐ ☐ 20 40 60 80 100
PSR62. Measuring and monitoring devices are used and controlled to ensure that measurement capability is consistent with the measurement requirements?		☐ ☐ ☐ ☐ ☐ 20 40 60 80 100
PSR63. Where applicable, measuring and monitoring devices: a.) are calibrated and adjusted periodically or prior to use, against devices traceable to international or national standards? b.) where no such standards exist, is the basis used for calibration recorded? c.) safeguarded from adjustments that would invalidate the calibration? d.) protected from damage and deterioration during handling, maintenance, and storage? e.) have the results of their calibration been recorded? f.) have the validity of previous results been reassessed if they are subsequently found out of calibration and corrective action taken?		☐ ☐ ☐ ☐ ☐ 20 40 60 80 100
PSR64. If software is used for measuring and monitoring of specified requirements software shall be validated prior to use?		☐ ☐ ☐ ☐ ☐ 20 40 60 80 100

ISO 9001:2000 Clause 8 – Measurement, Analysis and Improvement

	Documentation	Implementation
MAI1. Measurement and monitoring of activities needed to assure conformity and achieve improvement have been identified and included in the product/service delivery quality improvement plan?	❑ ❑ ❑ ❑ ❑ 20　40　60　80　100	
MAI2. Service delivery and production process should include the determination of the need for, and use of, applicable improvement methodologies including statistical techniques?	❑ ❑ ❑ ❑ ❑ 20　40　60　80　100	
MAI3. There are methods in place to understand customer perception related to meeting customer requirements?		❑ ❑ ❑ ❑ ❑ 20　40　60　80　100
MAI4. Customer perception is used as a measurement to determine the performance of the quality management system?		❑ ❑ ❑ ❑ ❑ 20　40　60　80　100
MAI5. Customer perception related to meeting customer requirements is documented and used as an input for decisions?	❑ ❑ ❑ ❑ ❑ 20　40　60　80　100	
MAI6. Periodic internal quality (tracer) audits of the organization's practices and processes are conducted to determine whether the quality management system has been effectively implemented and maintained?		❑ ❑ ❑ ❑ ❑ 20　40　60　80　100
MAI7. Internal quality (tracer) audits of the management system processes are planned, including consideration of the status and importance of the activities and areas to be audited as well as the results of previous audits?	❑ ❑ ❑ ❑ ❑ 20　40　60　80　100	
MAI8. The audit scope, frequency, and audit methodologies are defined?	❑ ❑ ❑ ❑ ❑ 20　40　60　80　100	
MAI9. Internal audits are conducted by personnel other than those who performed the activity being audited?		❑ ❑ ❑ ❑ ❑ 20　40　60　80　100
MAI10. A documented procedure is available that defines the responsibilities and requirements for conducting audits, ensuring their independence, recording results, and reporting to management?	❑ ❑ ❑ ❑ ❑ 20　40　60　80　100	
MAI11. Personnel conducting internal audits have been trained?		❑ ❑ ❑ ❑ ❑ 20　40　60　80　100
MAI12. Records of internal auditor training are maintained and available?	❑ ❑ ❑ ❑ ❑ 20　40　60　80　100	
MAI13. Management takes timely corrective action on deficiencies found during the audit?		❑ ❑ ❑ ❑ ❑ 20　40　60　80　100
MAI14. Follow-up actions include the verification of the implementation of corrective action taken?		❑ ❑ ❑ ❑ ❑ 20　40　60　80　100
MAI15. Service and product realization processes are measured and monitored by suitable methods to ensure customer requirements are met?		❑ ❑ ❑ ❑ ❑ 20　40　60　80　100

continued

ISO 9001:2000 Clause 8 – Measurement, Analysis and Improvement (*continued*)

	Documentation	Implementation
MAI16. These methods confirm the continuing ability of each process to satisfy its intended purpose?		❏ ❏ ❏ ❏ ❏ 20 40 60 80 100
MAI17. Service delivery and product characteristics are measured and monitored to verify that requirements for the product are met?		❏ ❏ ❏ ❏ ❏ 20 40 60 80 100
MAI18. Evidence of conformity with the acceptance criteria is documented?	❏ ❏ ❏ ❏ ❏ 20 40 60 80 100	
MAI19. Product, which does not conform to requirements is clearly identified and controlled to preventunintended use or delivery?		❏ ❏ ❏ ❏ ❏ 20 40 60 80 100
MAI20. Activities regarding service delivery that does not conform is defined in a documented procedure?	❏ ❏ ❏ ❏ ❏ 20 40 60 80 100	
MAI21. Non-conforming product is corrected and subjected to re-verification after correction to demonstrate conformity to requirements?	❏ ❏ ❏ ❏ ❏ 20 40 60 80 100	
MAI22. When non-conforming product is detected after delivery or use has started, appropriate action is taken regarding the consequences of the non-conformity?		❏ ❏ ❏ ❏ ❏ 20 40 60 80 100
MAI23. Appropriate data are collected and analyzed to determine the suitability and effectiveness of the quality management system and to identify improvements that can be made?		❏ ❏ ❏ ❏ ❏ 20 40 60 80 100
MAI24. Data are generated by measuring and monitoring activities and other relevant sources?	❏ ❏ ❏ ❏ ❏ 20 40 60 80 100	
MAI25. Appropriate data are collected and analyzed to determine the suitability and effectiveness of the quality management system and to identify improvements that can be made? Does this include data generated by measuring and monitoring activities and other relevant sources? How are these data analyzed to provide information on: a.) customer satisfaction and/or dissatisfaction? b.) conformance to customer requirements? c.) characteristics of processes, product, and their trends? d.) suppliers?		❏ ❏ ❏ ❏ ❏ 20 40 60 80 100
MAI26. Processes necessary for the continual improvement of the quality management system are planned, documented and managed?	❏ ❏ ❏ ❏ ❏ 20 40 60 80 100	
MAI27. Continual improvement of the quality management system is facilitated through the use of: a.) quality policy? b.) quality objectives? c.) audit results? d.) analysis of data? e.) corrective and preventive action ? f.) management review?	❏ ❏ ❏ ❏ ❏ 20 40 60 80 100	

continued

ISO 9001:2000 Clause 8 – Measurement, Analysis and Improvement (*continued*)

	Documentation					Implementation				
MAI28. Corrective action is taken to eliminate the cause of non-conformities in order to prevent recurrence?						❑ 20	❑ 40	❑ 60	❑ 80	❑ 100
MAI29. Corrective action taken is appropriate to the impact of the problems encountered?	❑ 20	❑ 40	❑ 60	❑ 80	❑ 100					
MAI30. A documented procedure for corrective action is available which defines requirements for: a.) identifying non-conformities (including customer complaints)? b.) determining the causes of non-conformity? c.) evaluating the need for actions to ensure that non-conformities do not recur? d.) determining and implementing the corrective action needed? e.)recording results of action taken? f.) reviewing corrective action taken?	❑ 20	❑ 40	❑ 60	❑ 80	❑ 100					
MAI31. The organization has identified preventive action to eliminate the causes of potential non-conformities to prevent occurrence?						❑ 20	❑ 40	❑ 60	❑ 80	❑ 100
MAI32. Preventive action measures taken are appropriate to the impact of the potential problems?						❑ 20	❑ 40	❑ 60	❑ 80	❑ 100
MAI33. A documented procedure for preventive action defines requirements for: a.) identifying potential non-conformities and their causes? b.) determining and ensuring the implementation of preventive action needed? c.) recording results of action taken? d) reviewing preventive action taken?	❑ 20	❑ 40	❑ 60	❑ 80	❑ 100					
MAI34. Procedures for preventive action ensure that relevant information on actions taken is submitted for management review?	❑ 20	❑ 40	❑ 60	❑ 80	❑ 100					

ISO 9001:2000
Section Scoring Sheet #1

	Documentation	Implementation
4 Quality Management System	QMS 1 _____ QMS 2 _____ QMS 3 _____ QMS 4 _____ QMS 5 _____ QMS 7 _____ QMS 8 _____ QMS 10 _____ QMS 11 _____ QMS 12 _____	QMS 6 _____ QMS 9 _____
'D' Score + 'I' Score = [_____] Total Section Score Divide the Section Score by 11 = [_____] Section Average Score	'D' Score _____	'I' Score _____
5 Management Responsibility	MR 4 _____ MR 6 _____ MR 8 _____ MR 12 _____ MR 13 _____	MR 1 _____ MR 2 _____ MR 3 _____ MR 5 _____ MR 7 _____ MR 9 _____ MR 10 _____ MR 11 _____ MR 14 _____
'D' Score + 'I' Score = [_____] Total Section Score Divide the Section Score by 14 [_____] Section Average Score	'D' Score _____	'I' Score _____
6 Resource Management	RM 1 _____ RM 4 _____	RM 2 _____ RM 3 _____ RM 5 _____ RM 6 _____ RM 7 _____ RM 8 _____
'D' Score + 'I' Score = [_____] Total Section Score Divide the Section Score by 8 [_____] Section Average Score	'D' Score _____	'I' Score _____

ISO 9001:2000
Section Scoring Sheet #2

Documentation	Implementation

7 Production and Service Delivery

'D' Score + 'I' Score = [　　　]
Total Section Score

Divide the Section Score by 64 = [　　　]
Section Average Score

Documentation	Implementation
PSR 2 _____	PSR 1 _____
PSR 3 _____	PSR 5 _____
PSR 4 _____	PSR 6 _____
PSR 8 _____	PSR 7 _____
PSR 9 _____	PSR 10 _____
PSR 13 _____	PSR 11 _____
PSR 14 _____	PSR 12 _____
PSR 15 _____	PSR 17 _____
PSR 16 _____	PSR 18 _____
PSR 20 _____	PSR 19 _____
PSR 21 _____	PSR 23 _____
PSR 22 _____	PSR 26 _____
PSR 24 _____	PSR 27 _____
PSR 25 _____	PSR 28 _____
PSR 29 _____	PSR 31 _____
PSR 30 _____	PSR 33 _____
PSR 32 _____	PSR 34 _____
PSR 36 _____	PSR 35 _____
PSR 39 _____	PSR 37 _____
PSR 42 _____	PSR 38 _____
PSR 43 _____	PSR 40 _____
PSR 49 _____	PSR 41 _____
PSR 50 _____	PSR 44 _____
PSR 51 _____	PSR 45 _____
PSR 52 _____	PSR 46 _____
PSR 57 _____	PSR 47 _____
PSR 60 _____	PSR 48 _____
	PSR 53 _____
	PSR 54 _____
	PSR 55 _____
	PSR 56 _____
	PSR 58 _____
	PSR 59 _____
	PSR 61 _____
	PSR 62 _____
	PSR 63 _____
	PSR 64 _____
'D' Score _____	'I' Score _____

ISO 9001:2000
Section Scoring Sheet #3

Documentation	Implementation

8 Measurement, Analysis and Improvement

'D' Score + 'I' Score =

Total Section Score

Divide the Section Score by 31

Section Average Score

Documentation	Implementation
MAI 1 _____	MAI 3 _____
MAI 2 _____	MAI 4 _____
MAI 5 _____	MAI 6 _____
MAI 7 _____	MAI 9 _____
MAI 8 _____	MAI 11 _____
MAI 10 _____	MAI 13 _____
MAI 12 _____	MAI 14 _____
MAI 18 _____	MAI 15 _____
MAI 20 _____	MAI 16 _____
MAI 21 _____	MAI 17 _____
MAI 24 _____	MAI 19 _____
MAI 26 _____	MAI 22 _____
MAI 27 _____	MAI 23 _____
MAI 29 _____	MAI 25 _____
MAI 30 _____	MAI 28 _____
MAI 31 _____	MAI 31 _____
MAI 33 _____	MAI 32 _____
MAI 34 _____	
'D' Score _____	'I' Score _____

FINAL SCORING SHEET

	Documentation	Implementation
	SECTION AVERAGE SCORE	

SCORE SHEET #1-
4. Quality Management System
5. Management Responsibility
6. Resource Management

_____
_____
_____

SCORE SHEET #2-
7. Production and Service Delivery

_____

SCORE SHEET #3-
8. Measurement, Analysis and Improvement

_____

ADD COLUMNS ABOVE & ENTER HERE   F   [_____]

DIVIDE TOTAL SCORE BY 5
This Score Represents Your % of Readiness For
ISO 9001:2000 Certification.   F   [_____ %]

Sample ISO 9001:2000 Quality Systems Manual and Procedures

SAMPLE QUALITY SYSTEMS MANUAL AND PROCEDURES

This appendix contains a sample manual and the six procedures required by ISO 9001:2000. The samples that follow are provided to allow the practice to begin the implementation process toward ISO 9001:2000 registration. It should be noted that the manual and procedures alone will not be enough for the health-care organization to meet all of the requirements of the ISO 9001:2000 standard nor will certification be granted by simply editing these documents and using them. The manual and procedures are examples only and provide a starting point for the organization.

It is highly recommended that assistance from qualified consultants be sought prior to actual implementation of the quality management system as other procedures in addition to those found in the appendix will be needed to be successful. When seeking guidance from consultants the health-care organization should consider two important factors: 1) that the firm providing consultation is ISO 9001:2000 certified itself, and 2) that the firm has worked with other IVF organizations assisting them achieve ISO 9001:2000 certification. There are thousands of consulting firms to choose from, but only a small handful that meet both of the criteria noted above.

Boston IVF

ISO 9001:2000
Quality Systems Manual

Boston IVF
40 Second Avenue
Waltham, Massachusetts 02451

Boston IVF / RI
6 Blackstone Valley Plaza, Suite 707
Lincoln, RI 02865

Boston IVF / Brookline
1 Brookline Place, Suite 600
Brookline, MA 02445

Boston IVF, The Woburn Center
23 Warren Avenue
Woburn, MA 01801

Boston IVF / Quincy
2300 Crown Colony Drive
Quincy, MA 02168

Boston IVF / Surgery Center of Waltham
40 Second Avenue
Waltham, Massachusetts 02451

Boston IVF

ISO 9001:2000
QUALITY SYSTEMS MANUAL

QM
Page 2 of 32
Issued: Initial Draft
Revised: 12/28/04
Supersedes: N/A

DOCUMENT AUTHORIZATION

Authorized Signature	Date
Authorized Signature	Date
Authorized Signature	Date
Authorized Signature	Date
Authorized Signature	Date
Authorized Signature	Date

Change Record

Rev. Date	Responsible Person	Description of Change

ISO 9001:2000
QUALITY SYSTEMS MANUAL

QM
Page 3 of 32
Issued: Initial Draft
Revised: 12/28/04
Supersedes: N/A

TABLE OF CONTENTS

1	Terms/definitions	Page 5
2	Scope	Page 6
3	Introduction	Page 8
4	Quality management system	Page 9
4.1	General requirements	Page 9
4.2	Documentation requirements	Page 10
4.2.1	General	Page 10
4.2.2	Quality manual	Page 10
4.2.3	Control of documents	Page 11
4.2.4	Control of records	Page 11
5	Management responsibility	Page 11
5.1	Management commitment	Page 11
5.2	Customer focus	Page 12
5.3	Quality policy	Page 13
5.4	Planning	Page 14
5.4.1	Quality objectives	Page 14
5.4.2	Quality planning	Page 14
5.5	Responsibility, authority and communication	Page 14
5.5.1	Responsibility and authority	Page 14
5.5.2	Management representative	Page 15
5.5.3	Internal communication	Page 15
5.6	Management review	Page 15
5.6.1	General	Page 15
5.6.2	Review input	Page 15
5.6.3	Review output	Page 16
6	Resource management	Page 16
6.1	Provision of resources	Page 16
6.2	Human resources	Page 16
6.2.1	General	Page 16
6.6.2	Competence, awareness and training	Page 16
6.3	Infrastructure	Page 16
6.4	Work environment	Page 17
7	Product realization	Page 17
7.1	Planning of product realization	Page 17
7.2	Customer-related processes	Page 17
7.2.1	Determination of requirements related to the product	Page 17

Boston IVF

ISO 9001:2000
QUALITY SYSTEMS MANUAL

QM
Page 4 of 32

Issued: Initial Draft
Revised: 12/28/04
Supersedes: N/A

7.2.2	Review of customer requirements	Page 18
7.2.3	Customer communication	Page 18
7.3	Design and/or development	Page 19
7.3.1	Design and/or development planning	Page 19
7.3.2	Design and/or development inputs	Page 19
7.3.3	Design and/or development outputs	Page 19
7.3.4	Design and/or development review	Page 20
7.3.5	Design and/or development verification	Page 20
7.3.6	Design and/or development validation	Page 20
7.3.7	Control of design and/or development changes	Page 20
7.4	Purchasing	Page 21
7.4.1	General requirements	Page 21
7.4.2	Purchasing information	Page 21
7.4.3	Verification of purchased product	Page 22
7.5	Production and service provision	Page 22
7.5.1	Control of operations	Page 22
7.5.2	Validation of processes	Page 22
7.5.3	Identification and traceability	Page 22
7.5.4	Customer property	Page 23
7.5.5	Preservation of product	Page 23
7.6	Control of measuring and monitoring devices	Page 25
8	Measurement, analysis and improvement	Page 26
8.1	Planning	Page 26
8.2	Measurement and monitoring	Page 26
8.2.1	Patient/customer satisfaction	Page 26
8.2.2	Internal audit	Page 27
8.2.3	Measurement and monitoring of processes and products	Page 27
8.3	Control of non-conformity	Page 27
8.4	Analysis of data	Page 28
8.5	Improvement	Page 29
8.5.1	Planning for continual improvement	Page 29
8.5.2	Corrective action	Page 29
8.5.3	Preventive action	Page 29
Addendum 1:	System Procedures	Page 30

Boston IVF

ISO 9001:2000
QUALITY SYSTEMS MANUAL

QM
Page 5 of 32
Issued: Initial Draft
Revised: 12/28/04
Supersedes: N/A

1 Terms/Definitions

AH	Assisted hatching
ART	Assisted reproductive technologies
BIVF	Boston IVF
CC	Clomiphene citrate
CCT	Clomiphene Challenge Test
E2	Estradiol
EEJ	Electro-ejaculation
ET	Embryo transfer
GIFT	Gamete intrafallopian transfer
GNRHa	Gonadotropin releasing hormone agonist
FSH	Follicle stimulating hormone
hCG	Human chorionic gonadotropin
hMG	Human menopausal gonadotropin (Pergonal®)
HSA	Human serum albumin
ICSI	Intracytoplasmic sperm injection
IM	Intramuscularly
IUI	Intrauterine insemination
LH	Luteinizing hormone
LOR	Laparoscopic oocyte retrieval
OHSS	Ovarian hyperstimulation syndrome
OR	Operating room
P4	Progesterone
RE	Reproductive Endocrinologist
r-FSH	Recombinant FSH
SAB	Spontaneous abortion
SC	Subcutaneously
TET	Tubal embryo transfer
uFSH	Urinary FSH (Metrodin®)
UT	Uterine transfer
US	Ultrasound
VOR	Vaginal oocyte retrieval

Boston IVF

ISO 9001:2000
QUALITY SYSTEMS MANUAL

QM
Page 6 of 32
Issued: Initial Draft
Revised: 12/28/04
Supersedes: N/A

2 Scope

This manual describes the quality system requirements for services provided by Boston IVF.

Boston IVF is a highly specialized outpatient fertility and *in vitro* fertilization center specifically devoted to the design and delivery of care for infertile couples and individuals. The core of our company's mission is to provide infertility services in a compassionate and responsive fashion in six offices.

Boston IVF
40 Second Avenue
Waltham, Massachusetts 02451

The central facility for Boston IVF is in Waltham, Massachusetts. The administrative functions of the quality management system are performed here, with process links to the entire system. Services offered at Waltham include:

- Consultation and evaluation
- General fertility treatment
- Ovulation stimulation cycles
- Ultrasound services
- Blood hormone evaluations
- Specimen collections
- Intrauterine inseminations
- IVF orientations and injection lessons
- IVF cycle monitoring
- Male infertility services
- Egg and sperm donation programs
- Counseling
- Andrology and Embryology Laboratories

Boston IVF / Surgery Center of Waltham
40 Second Avenue
Waltham, Massachusetts 02451

The "Surgery Center of Waltham", a division of BIVF housed in the same facility in Waltham, is an outpatient surgical facility that houses the surgical suites where all IVF cases are performed. Other outpatient surgical procedures such as laparoscopies and hysteroscopies are also performed at the Surgical Center.

Boston IVF

ISO 9001:2000
QUALITY SYSTEMS MANUAL

QM
Page 7 of 32
Issued: Initial Draft
Revised: 12/28/04
Supersedes: N/A

Supporting this facility are several centers throughout New England where BIVF clinicians care for patients closer to their own community. Services provided at these centers include:

- Consultation and evaluation
- General fertility treatment
- Ovulation and stimulation cycles
- Ultrasound services
- Blood hormone evaluations
- Specimen collections
- Intrauterine inseminations
- IVF orientations and injection lessons
- IVF cycle monitoring
- Counseling

Boston IVF

ISO 9001:2000
QUALITY SYSTEMS MANUAL

QM
Page 8 of 32
Issued: Initial Draft
Revised: 12/28/04
Supersedes: N/A

3   Introduction

Boston IVF is a highly specialized outpatient fertility and *in vitro* fertilization center specifically devoted to the care of infertile couples and individuals. It is our mission to use our clinical and scientific skills, plus our strong sense of empathy and compassion, to deliver the very best in reproductive therapies to the patients we serve.

As the first self-contained outpatient fertility center in the United States, Boston IVF has a distinguished place in the history of assisted reproduction. In New England, we were responsible for the first birth resulting from the gamete intrafallopian transfer (GIFT) procedure, as well as the first birth from intracytoplasmic sperm injection (ICSI). Today, both procedures are widely performed, thanks in part to the pioneering efforts of Boston IVF clinicians and scientists.

With one of the nation's largest groups of reproductive medicine specialists, Boston IVF has been instrumental in the birth of over 7,500 babies. We are privileged to offer our patients the best of both worlds; the most advanced treatments available in the private, confidential setting of our conveniently located fertility centers.

At the core of BIVF are the gifted and talented clinicians. The clinicians are specialty trained reproductive endocrinologists with extensive experience in reproductive medicine. Nursing and support services rank as one of the most experienced in the field.

Teaching and education are important missions for BIVF. BIVF forms the division of reproductive endocrinology at the Beth Israel Deaconess Medical Center and Harvard Medical School in Boston, Massachusetts. Fellows, residents, and medical students lend to the vibrant academic atmosphere at BIVF.

Research has been a longstanding focus for our scientists and clinicians. Industry and government sponsored investigations are managed by a research coordinator and support staff under the direction of the Director of Research, Division Chief, and Scientific Director. The clinical volume offers a unique opportunity to answer important clinical questions.

A strong administrative team and an ISO 9001:2000 quality management system is in place to allow for the clinical, teaching and research missions to be accomplished.

Boston IVF

ISO 9001:2000
QUALITY SYSTEMS MANUAL

QM
Page 9 of 32
Issued: Initial Draft
Revised: 12/28/04
Supersedes: N/A

4   Quality management system

4.1   General requirements

Boston IVF has established, documented, and implemented a quality management system in accordance with the requirements of ISO 9001:2000. The system is maintained and its effectiveness is evaluated and improved on a continuous basis.

a) Processes in the quality management system are identified and applied; to achieve consistency in service delivery and to provide compassionate, appropriate care to each patient the process not only identifies important process steps but also identifies customization points where individual needs are considered and addressed.

b) The sequence and interaction of processes in the quality management system follow:

c) Work criteria are determined and methods are defined for processes. Processes are controlled and evaluated to ensure that they remain effective.

d) Resources and information that are necessary to support operations are available. Resources and information needed for monitoring all processes are also available.

e) Processes are monitored, measured and analyzed.

f) Actions that are necessary to achieve planned results are implemented. Actions necessary to achieve continual improvement of processes are also implemented.

Boston IVF ensures that services delivered comply with customer requirements and expectations by defining and managing service delivery processes. Boston IVF's quality management system addresses all requirements and elements of the ISO 9001:2000 standard. This quality system also meets or exceeds the requirements of the College of American Pathologists, HCFA, State of Massachusetts Department of Public Health, SART, the CDC and AAAHC.

Where services are outsourced, Boston IVF defines control over the processes in the quality management system. Controls are typically inspection upon receipt when possible, or requirements defined by contractual agreement.

Boston IVF

ISO 9001:2000
QUALITY SYSTEMS MANUAL

QM
Page 10 of 32
Issued: Initial Draft
Revised: 12/28/04
Supersedes: N/A

4.2   Documentation requirements

4.2.1 General

Quality management system documents at BOSTON IVF include:

a) Quality policy and quality objectives. These are quality documents that are approved and controlled, with their own document numbers. One quality policy governs the entire quality management system; quality objectives are established in accordance with section 5.4.1 of this manual.

b) Quality manual. This document describes the elements and scope of Boston IVF's quality management system. It is the statement of policy for the entire system.

c) System procedures required by ISO 9001:2000. These required procedures include:

- Document control
- Control of records
- Internal audits
- Control of non-conformance
- Corrective action
- Preventive action

Other procedures that apply across the entire company may be defined as system procedures in addition to the required list above.

d) Documents needed at Boston IVF to ensure effective planning, operation and control of all processes. These documents include clinical and non-clinical procedures, work instructions, and forms.

e) Records to provide evidence of conformity to requirements. Records may be electronic or hard copy; maintained on forms or in databases.

4.2.2 Quality manual

The quality manual includes the scope of the quality management system. No exclusions apply. Procedures are referenced in Addendum I, referenced here and published with the manual. The processes in the system and their interaction are described in Addendum II, also published with the manual.

Boston IVF

ISO 9001:2000
QUALITY SYSTEMS MANUAL

QM
Page 11 of 32
Issued: Initial Draft
Revised: 12/28/04
Supersedes: N/A

4.2.3 Control of documents

Documents required in the quality management system are controlled in accordance with the Document Control Procedure. Records are controlled in accordance with 4.2.4.

Controls are defined for:
a) Approving documents prior to issuance
b) Reviewing and updating documents and re-approving documents
c) Identifying changes and revision status of documents
d) Ensuring that relevant versions of applicable documents are available at points of use
e) Ensuring that documents are legible and identifiable
f) Ensuring that documents of external origin are identified and their distribution controlled
g) Preventing the unintended use of obsolete documents; identifying them when they are retained.

4.2.4 Control of records

Records are evidence that requirements were met. They show that the quality system is operating effectively. Such records are defined and maintained in accordance with the Control of Records Procedure. Each procedure and/or protocol defines which records are kept for the activity described. The Control of Records Procedure contains a master list of all records.

Records are legible, readily identifiable and retrievable.

The Control of Records Procedure defines controls for:
- Identification
- Storage
- Protection
- Retrieval
- Retention time
- Disposition of records.

5 Management responsibility

5.1 Management commitment

Top management for the quality management system is defined as:
- Medical Director

Boston IVF

ISO 9001:2000
QUALITY SYSTEMS MANUAL

QM
Page 12 of 32
Issued: Initial Draft
Revised: 12/28/04
Supersedes: N/A

- Chief Operations Officer
- Chief Financial Officer
- Director of Nursing
- Director of Operating Room/Post Anesthesia Care Unit (OR/PACU)
- Director of Ultrasound
- Director of Billing
- Director of HR
- Director of Lab
- Director of Marketing
- IT Director
- Data Entry Supervisor
- Contracts Manager

Top management ensures that awareness of the customers' requirements is maintained throughout the organization; establishes quality management systems requirements, quality policy, quality objectives, and quality planning; establishes, maintains and continuously improves the quality management system; performs management reviews of the quality management system, and ensures that proper resources are available.

Management commitment to the development and improvement of the quality system is demonstrated through the implementation of this quality system, evidenced by quality records.

5.2   Customer focus

BOSTON IVF has multiple customers. Customers are both internal and external to the company; "internal customers" describes the interaction of employees and departments as work is performed on a daily basis. Interaction between physicians and other staff, for example, puts the physician in the role of customer, receiving service from the quality system. External customers include patients who receive services directly, and insurance companies whose requirements must be satisfied in order to receive payment for those services that are rendered.

While it is possible to conclude that customers may be any individual who could benefit from our services and ultimately society at large, the focus of this quality management system is on the following critical customer relationships:

- **Patients:** *manage their expectations in the area of clinical outcomes, then provide service within those managed expectations that provides satisfaction*
- **Internal customers** throughout the quality management system: *provide timely, accurate information and service with good working relationships. Includes employee physicians*

Boston IVF

ISO 9001:2000
QUALITY SYSTEMS MANUAL

QM
Page 13 of 32
Issued: Initial Draft
Revised: 12/28/04
Supersedes: N/A

- **Referring physicians:** *offer the latest technological capability, build trusting relationships, offer ease and accuracy in sharing information. Includes referring OB/GYN's, Urologists*
- **Medical community:** *clinical services and research; point of training; expand the knowledge base in the field*
- **Insurance providers:** *provide accurate information with knowledge of their requirements, cost-effective service*
- **Residents:** *receive training and provide service for patients*

Top management is responsible to ensure that customer requirements are determined. They oversee the effort of the entire quality management system to meet customer requirements and enhance customer satisfaction.

5.3   Quality policy

Boston IVF has adopted a quality policy. The statement is as follows:

The quality policy is posted throughout the facility, has been endorsed by employees, and approved by Top Management.

The quality policy is communicated to all employees through newsletters, staff meetings, training opportunities, and other appropriate forums. All employees are encouraged and required to embrace this policy.

Top Management has the responsibility to ensure that Boston IVF's quality policy...

- Is relevant to the nature of services provided by the organization and to the needs and expectations of its customers;
- Underscores the organization's commitment to meeting applicable requirements and standards;
- Underscores the organization's dedication to continual quality improvement;
- Provides a framework for establishing and reviewing the organization's quality goals and objectives;
- Is communicated, understood and implemented at all levels of the organization;
- Is reviewed on a regular basis for continuing suitability and relevance to the overall purpose of the organization.

The quality policy is a controlled document.

Boston IVF

ISO 9001:2000
QUALITY SYSTEMS MANUAL

QM
Page 14 of 32
Issued: Initial Draft
Revised: 12/28/04
Supersedes: N/A

5.4 Planning

5.4.1 Quality objectives

Top Management oversees the process of establishing quality objectives for BOSTON IVF. The quality objectives reflect our customer focus as well as our commitment to top quality service. Quality objectives are measurable; they are established at relevant functions and levels in the organization; they support the quality policy.

5.4.2 Quality planning

Quality planning is initiated at multiple levels in the quality management system.

Top Management coordinates budgeting of funds, determining staffing needs, identifying needs for equipment, processes, and any other resources needed to achieve the desired results.

Establishing/revising procedures and protocols also constitutes quality planning. At this level, quality planning covers:

- Processes including criteria and methods required for the quality management system;
- Identification of interactions and resources needed to achieve desired results;
- Identification of quality requirements at defined stages of service delivery;
- Verification activities such as quality audits and reporting;
- Identification and control of necessary quality records;
- Requirements for implementing actions for improvement.

Planning controls organizational and process changes and ensures that the quality management system is maintained at all times.

Regulatory requirements that apply to the services provided by the organization are identified as an integral part of all quality planning activities.

5.5 Responsibility, authority and communication

5.5.1 Responsibility and authority

Responsibility and authority for quality management including all activities that affect quality are defined in the organizational chart and job descriptions.

Boston IVF

ISO 9001:2000
QUALITY SYSTEMS MANUAL

QM
Page 15 of 32
Issued: Initial Draft
Revised: 12/28/04
Supersedes: N/A

5.5.2 Management representative

The Management Representative has the authority and responsibility to ensure that the requirements of this Quality Systems Manual and of the entire Quality Management System are implemented, maintained and continuously improved. The Management Representative communicates with Top Management regarding the performance of the quality management system including needs for improvement.

The Management Representative is responsible for promoting awareness of customer requirements throughout all levels of the organization.

5.5.3 Internal communication

Top Management meets with the Management Representative at least monthly to address issues regarding the effectiveness of the quality management system. Issues related to patients are reported immediately and addressed according to their perceived impact.

5.6   Management review

5.6.1 General

Top Management reviews the quality system at least annually to assure that compliance with ISO 9001:2000 and applicable regulations is maintained and continuous improvement is accomplished. The focus of the review is to ensure continuing suitability, adequacy and effectiveness of the system. Opportunities for improvement, the need for change to the system, and re-evaluation of the quality policy and quality objectives are assessed and records maintained.

5.6.2 Review input

Top Management reviews:

- Customer feedback
- Results of internal audits and regulatory audits/surveys
- Measures of processes and outcomes
- Status and results of corrective and preventive actions
- Follow-up actions from previous management reviews
- Changes that could affect the quality management system
- Recommendations for improvement

Boston IVF

ISO 9001:2000
QUALITY SYSTEMS MANUAL

QM
Page 16 of 32
Issued: Initial Draft
Revised: 12/28/04
Supersedes: N/A

5.6.3 Review output

Outputs from these reviews include actions designed to improve the effectiveness of the quality management system, actions related to improving the provision of service to meet customer requirements, and actions related to providing resources.

6   Resource management

6.1   *Provision of resources*

Resources are provided in order to establish and maintain Boston IVF's quality management system and to satisfy customers.

6.2 *Human resources*

6.2.1 General

Human Resources is responsible to verify competency of employees with defined responsibility in the Quality Management System on the basis of education, training, skills and experience. Only employees who are deemed competent are assigned responsibilities in the Quality Management System.

6.2.2 Competence, awareness and training

Based on organizational responsibilities Boston IVF:

- Determines training needs and requirements for competency;
- Provides training when a need is identified or takes an action to satisfy the need;
- Evaluates effectiveness of training or of the action taken;
- Ensures that employees are aware of their role in the achievement of quality goals and objectives;
- Maintains records for education, training, skills, and experience.

6.3   *Infrastructure*

Infrastructure for the Boston IVF includes workspaces and facilities; equipment (including hardware and software); suitable maintenance; and supporting services. The infrastructure required for service delivery is determined, provided, and maintained.

Boston IVF

ISO 9001:2000
QUALITY SYSTEMS MANUAL

QM
Page 17 of 32
Issued: Initial Draft
Revised: 12/28/04
Supersedes: N/A

6.4 Work environment

The work environment is managed to ensure conformity of service delivery. For example, where necessary, air quality is monitored and controlled so that appropriate environmental conditions are maintained for an operating room and embryology laboratory; light levels are appropriate to prevent damage to embryos; patient areas are kept at comfortable temperatures, etc.

7 Product realization

7.1 Planning of product realization

Boston IVF identifies, plans and implements processes necessary to realize requirements for service delivery. Quality System Procedures describe the sequence and interaction of activities and provide reference to applicable Procedures, Protocols and forms. Outputs from quality planning are considered when identifying needed processes. While the company has established overall objectives, these are specific to a particular activity and are the basis for assessing the quality of service delivered.

In planning process realization (generating procedures/protocols), each department at Boston IVF:

- Determines quality objectives and requirements for the product/service delivered (the activity described in the document);
- Determines what documents are used, what resources are needed (equipment, qualifications for providers, etc.), and the method (stepwise procedure);
- Determines which required verification, validation, monitoring, inspection and test activities will be required and the criteria for acceptance (Quality controls);
- Determines what records are needed to provide evidence that the process and resulting product meet requirements.

The output of planning is the documented procedure/protocol/form or database.

7.2 Customer-related processes

7.2.1 Determination of requirements related to the product

Boston IVF delivers infertility services. Requirements for the product are determined to be characteristics or requirements for service delivery.

Boston IVF

ISO 9001:2000
QUALITY SYSTEMS MANUAL

QM
Page 18 of 32
Issued: Initial Draft
Revised: 12/28/04
Supersedes: N/A

Customer requirements are established by the following methods:

Patients: Physician's initial and subsequent consultations and subsequent testing determine clinical and psychological requirements

Internal customer requirements are defined in procedures/protocols

Insurance companies/payers: Requirements are defined by contract

Customers are often multiple for any particular service, and all requirements must be met for patients, regulatory agencies, and other stakeholders.

7.2.2 Review of customer requirements

Patient requirements are reviewed before services are provided. This review is performed after the initial consult, when the medical assistant creates the patient chart and at various points in the delivery of service. Physician's orders are reviewed, patient consents are signed, insurance requirements are reviewed by the financial coordinator at various points in the delivery of service, discussion of expected outcomes and possible complications with the patient are held and recorded.

Contracts with insurance providers, contracted physicians, residents are reviewed prior to delivery of service.

Commitments are reviewed to ensure that:

- Requirements are clearly defined;
- All requirements are confirmed by the patient/customer before their acceptance;
- Differences between the service requirements of the patient/customer and the care provider are reconciled and resolved prior to performing the service;
- The organization has the ability to meet requirements for service as requested.

Both the results of the review of agreements and any follow-up actions are recorded. Where service requirements are changed either by the patient/customer and/or the service provider, documentation may be amended and all relevant personnel are made aware of the changed requirements.

7.2.3 Customer communication

In order to meet customer requirements, Boston IVF has established arrangements for communication with patients/customers. Communication arrangements address the following aspects:

- Information about services provided and impact of services;
- Information related to modification of any service to be provided;

Boston IVF

ISO 9001:2000
QUALITY SYSTEMS MANUAL

QM
Page 19 of 32
Issued: Initial Draft
Revised: 12/28/04
Supersedes: N/A

- Information related to customer complaints and actions in response to non-conforming service;
- Patient/customer feedback about acceptability of service.

7.3 Design and/or development

7.3.1 Design and/or development planning

Documented procedures are maintained to plan and control research and development.

Design and development planning procedures include:

- Stages of the development process;
- Required reviews;
- Verification and validation activities;
- Responsibilities and authorities for research and development activities.

Interfaces between different groups involved in the design and development are managed so that communication is clear and effective and design responsibilities are understood. Planning outputs are updated as appropriate as the care plan design and development evolves.

7.3.2 Design and/or development inputs

As part of the care plan design and development process, applicable requirements are identified, defined and properly recorded. These documented requirements include:

- Standards of identified patient/customer needs;
- Applicable regulatory and legal requirements;
- Requirements from previous similar designs;
- Input from associates and physician practice guidelines;
- Other requirements required for development

All requirements are reviewed for adequacy. Requirements that appear to be incomplete, ambiguous or conflicting are resolved.

7.3.3 Design and/or development outputs

Outputs or outcomes of the development process are recorded so that they can be compared to the input requirements. Development outcomes must:
- Meet input requirements;
- Provide necessary information to ensure effective health care delivery to the patient;

Boston IVF

ISO 9001:2000
QUALITY SYSTEMS MANUAL

QM
Page 20 of 32
Issued: Initial Draft
Revised: 12/28/04
Supersedes: N/A

- Define goals of the care plan that are essential to health and safety of the patient/customer.

Design output documents are approved before release.

7.3.4 Design and/or development review

Systematic reviews are planned and conducted at suitable stages in the design and/or development process. These reviews evaluate the content and effectiveness of the care plan in order to direct the interventions and expected patient outcomes.

Representatives from all relevant functions involved at the applicable stage of development participate in the review. Records are maintained of the review and subsequent follow-up actions.

7.3.5 Design and/or development verification

Design verification at Boston IVF is performed as part of design review. The purpose of design review and design verification is to ensure consistency between design input and output. Results of verification and any follow-up are recorded.

7.3.6   Design and/or development validation

Validation confirms that the design is capable of meeting the outcome requirements specified. When possible, validation is undertaken prior to implementation. The results of design validation and any follow-up activities are recorded.

7.3.7 Control of design and/or development changes

Modifications to the design are approved by authorized personnel and recorded before implementation.

Developer(s) determine the effect of changes on:

- The evaluation of the effect of changes in order to promote a positive outcome;
- The interaction between care plan components that affect patient care delivery;
- The need for re-verification or re-validation for the program or outcomes.

Modification of age specific lesson plans and follow-up actions are recorded and approved by authorized personnel and recorded before implementation.

Boston IVF

ISO 9001:2000
QUALITY SYSTEMS MANUAL

QM
Page 21 of 32
Issued: Initial Draft
Revised: 12/28/04
Supersedes: N/A

7.4   Purchasing

7.4.1 General requirements

Boston IVF has documented and implemented procedures to ensure that all medical products, supplies and services purchased conform to specified requirements. The type and extent of control exercised over vendors is identified in documented procedures. Vendors, suppliers and subcontractors are evaluated and selected based on their ability to supply products/services in accordance with Boston IVF's established policies and procedures.

Vendors are selected based upon:

- Reputation of the vendor;
- Ability to deliver in a timely manner;
- Quality of products and services;
- Competitive pricing;
- Professional qualifications and/or proof of insurance where applicable for sub-contracted services and/or certifications.

Periodic evaluations are performed. Results of evaluations and subsequent follow-up actions are recorded.

7.4.2 Purchasing information

Purchasing documents clearly describe the product or service ordered including any associated requirements. The requirements needed for approval, qualification of product, procedures, processes, equipment and personnel requirements are defined.

Purchasing documents are reviewed and approved prior to release except where purchases are authorized as described below:

- Boston IVF credit cards are issued to authorized employees. These purchases are controlled by approved spending limits per purchase and total card limits. Use of these cards is governed by policy.
- Employees may make purchases on their own credit, and submit receipts for reimbursement.
- Petty cash purchases are controlled by issuance of receipts documenting the item(s) purchased, and dollar amount(s). Procedures determine amount available and documentation required.

Boston IVF

ISO 9001:2000
QUALITY SYSTEMS MANUAL

QM
Page 22 of 32
Issued: Initial Draft
Revised: 12/28/04
Supersedes: N/A

7.4.3 Verification of purchased product

Purchased items are subjected to receiving inspection to verify that the purchase received complies with stated requirements. If Boston IVF desires to perform a vendor audit, arrangements for this requirement are specified on the Purchase Order or other purchase documents.

7.5   Production and service provision (operation control)

7.5.1 Control of operations

Processes are planned and controlled. This control includes:

- The availability of information that describes the characteristics of the product;
- Clear work instructions (procedures/protocols) as necessary;
- The use of suitable equipment;
- The availability and use of suitable measuring and monitoring equipment;
- The implementation of suitable monitoring and measurement;
- Implementing defined processes for release, delivery and post-delivery activities.

7.5.2 Validation of processes

Certain processes at Boston IVF cannot be verified until the process is fully implemented. (For example IVF, IVI). Therefore, Boston IVF ensures that licensed and/or accredited personnel (physicians, nurses) are appointed to develop and/or carry out these services. Where appropriate, these services are continuously monitored to ensure that specified standards of care are met. Validation of processes demonstrates the organization's ability to achieve planned outcomes.

Validation activities include the following:
- Qualification of personnel;
- Use of appropriate authorized procedures and protocols.

7.5.3 Identification and traceability

Patients are identified and tracked throughout service delivery by:
- the use of first and last names and dates of birth for patients;
- the assignment of a medical record number that identifies each patient.

Records of traceability, when applicable, are maintained.

Boston IVF

ISO 9001:2000
QUALITY SYSTEMS MANUAL

QM
Page 23 of 32
Issued: Initial Draft
Revised: 12/28/04
Supersedes: N/A

7.5.4 Customer property

Patient property is defined as any item brought to the Center by the patient or their family.

- Remind valuables should not be brought
- Valuables that are brought are secured under lock and key until removal by the patient
- Clothing is kept in patient lockers
- Assistive devices remain with the patient
- Medications are stored with valuables under lock and key

Fresh embryos and gametes are identified by female patient name and date of birth at all stages of processing.

Embryos produced during IVF procedures which are not transferred to the patient that are suitable for cryopreservation are stored in liquid nitrogen on site at Boston IVF. Storage is indefinite with accompanying charges for service. Embryos are identified by patient name and date of birth. Locations are identified per container. Computerized and hard copy database maintains traceability.

Homologous Sperm is identified by male patient name and date of birth on the individual vial and the cane. Storage is indefinite with accompanying charges for service. Locations are identified per container. Computerized database maintains traceability.

Purchased donor sperm is identified by donor bank designation on the vial, by the female patient name on the cane. The computerized database maintains record of both patient name and date of birth and the donor bank designation.

Any such item that is lost, damaged, or is otherwise unsuitable for use is recorded and reported to the patient.

7.5.5 Preservation of product

Care of Patients

Patients/customers are handled and transported in accordance with hospital Policies and Procedures. Employees are trained in proper techniques for the care of patients in various environments and health care delivery situations. This care includes issues related to the environment and care as well as safety and patients' rights.

ISO 9001:2000
QUALITY SYSTEMS MANUAL

Boston IVF

QM
Page 24 of 32
Issued: Initial Draft
Revised: 12/28/04
Supersedes: N/A

Transportation of Patients

Where legally or contractually specified, BOSTON IVF is responsible for the welfare of patients until transfer of responsibility.

Service Processes

Specific training provided for the care of patients in service processes includes:

- Recipient rights
- CPR and first aid (as applicable)
- Universal precautions
- Safe work practices
- Behavioral management plans (as applicable)
- Physical/non-physical management (as applicable)
- Specialized care needs applicable to specific patients
- Various topics as determined by program needs

Employees are trained in the proper handling, maintenance and storage of materials. Training is provided in the following areas:

- Blood-borne pathogens (BBP)
- Medication administration (as applicable)
- Right to know (Material Safety Data Sheet; MSDS)

Medical Supplies

Boston IVF Policies and Procedures ensure that all supplies are identified, handled, packaged, stored and protected to maintain the integrity of the purchased products.

Storage of supplies

Designated storage areas are used to protect materials from damage or deterioration as applicable prior to use or delivery. Storage areas are secured to prevent damage or deterioration of product, pending use or delivery. Medications and hazardous materials are secured in locked storage areas/cabinets. Only authorized persons have access to keys for these areas. The condition of stored product is regularly assessed as appropriate.

Storage of biological material

Boston IVF protocols define methods for identification, handling, packaging, storage and protection to maintain the integrity of the material.

Boston IVF

ISO 9001:2000
QUALITY SYSTEMS MANUAL

QM
Page 25 of 32
Issued: Initial Draft
Revised: 12/28/04
Supersedes: N/A

Packaging

Items are packaged to survive transportation and handling environments (i.e. sterile products and packs, storage bins, liquid nitrogen containers, etc.). Factors considered include fragility, environment conditions, mode of shipment, expected length of storage. Training is provided in the proper packaging, packing, and storage of materials.

Preservation

Appropriate methods of preserving and segregating medical products and supplies are implemented and communicated.

Delivery of Materials, Equipment and Lab Specimens

Where specified, BOSTON IVF is responsible for packaging and preservation of products during transit including delivery to destination.

7.6   Control of measuring and monitoring devices

Controls are established to maintain the integrity of equipment and devices used in measuring, and testing of patients, tests, lab results, imaging, etc.

Each department coordinates the scheduling, calibration, and inspection of measuring and testing devices to ensure conformity to specifications so that required measurement capability is known and is consistent with measurement requirements.

Calibration is traceable to national standards:

- Boston IVF has access to individual calibration records of all inspection, measurement, and test device as Quality Records.
- New equipment is registered and calibrated prior to use for inspection, measurement, and testing.
- Inspection, measuring and test equipment is identified and calibrated at prescribed intervals.
- Boston IVF provides employees with training in the handling, storage, and use of inspection, measurement, and test equipment, where required, so that improper handling does not invalidate the calibration settings.
- Safeguards against inadvertent adjustments to equipment are used when applicable.
- Any product that has been tested using out-of-tolerance inspection measurement and test equipment is re-inspected and Corrective Action is taken.

Boston IVF

ISO 9001:2000
QUALITY SYSTEMS MANUAL

QM
Page 26 of 32
Issued: Initial Draft
Revised: 12/28/04
Supersedes: N/A

Boston IVF ensures that:

- Measurements to be made and the accuracy required are determined;
- Appropriate inspection, measuring and test device and/or testing instruments capable of the necessary accuracy are used;
- Inspection, measuring and test equipment is identified and calibrated at prescribed intervals;
- Equipment used for calibration is traceable to National Institute of Standards and Technology (NIST);
- Calibration records contain details of calibration process used, type of equipment, identification, location, frequency of checks, acceptance criteria, action taken to adjust the instrument;
- Calibration stickers or calibration records identify calibration status;
- Records are maintained;
- When equipment is found to be out of calibration, previous test results using the instrument are assessed to determine validity;
- Suitable environmental conditions exist for the calibration being carried out;
- Accuracy and fitness for use of the device is maintained by proper handling and storage;
- Facilities and device are safeguarded from adjustments that would invalidate the calibration setting.

8 Measurement, analysis and improvement

8.1 Planning

Boston IVF strives to maintain excellence at all levels of interaction with patients. Boston IVF is a leader in research in infertility as well as maintaining a high standard of excellence in the laboratory. To support this effort toward continued improvement using the highest standards, Boston IVF monitors all aspects of the quality management system, implementing a plan for measurement, analysis and improvement to demonstrate conformity of service delivery, to ensure that the quality management system functions effectively, and to continually improve the quality management system.

8.2 Measurement and monitoring

8.2.1 Patient/customer satisfaction

Boston IVF has established processes for measurement, monitoring and review of information related to the performance level of the organization. Boston IVF has a system to identify, quantify and qualify Customers levels of satisfaction with the organization's services. This system includes surveys at various points of the service provision continuum, questionnaires and other inquiry formats. The system is designed to generate information that can be used for immediate modification of planned services, for modification of the structure of the organization's service components, for long-term planning and for continual improvement of the organization's service delivery system.

Boston IVF

ISO 9001:2000
QUALITY SYSTEMS MANUAL

QM
Page 27 of 32
Issued: Initial Draft
Revised: 12/28/04
Supersedes: N/A

8.2.2 Internal audit

Boston IVF has a program to audit its Quality System on a regular basis. The internal audit schedule for the various activities is established in accordance with the significance and impact that the audited activities have on the overall Quality System and in accordance with the results of previous internal audits. The assignment of auditors also ensures that auditors are independent of the activity audited. Each segment of the system and component of the Quality System is audited at least annually.

Boston IVF maintains a system level procedure that outlines the scope, frequency and methodology of its internal audits. This procedure also establishes the terms of eligibility and responsibility for internal audits and the mechanism for reporting of audit results to appropriate management personnel.

8.2.3 Measurement and monitoring of processes and product requirements

Realization processes (implementation of policies/work instructions) are monitored or measured by an appropriate indicator (quality objectives) to ensure that requirements are met. It is more important to choose the right indicator than to monitor every activity; a carefully chosen indicator measures all prior activities to determine the suitability and effectiveness of the processes. These methods for and records of measurement and monitoring confirm that processes are suitable to satisfy their purpose.

Since the business of Boston IVF is the delivery of service, monitoring the process is not distinct and separate from monitoring the product.

Outcomes indicators are reported in various formats such as SART reporting, pregnancy rates and fertility rates; these are benchmarked against industry standards. These may be significant indicators within the industry, but are not defined in this quality system as critical quality measurements related to customer satisfaction.

8.3 Control of non-conformity

Boston IVF has established methods to collect information related to the effectiveness and output of processes used in service delivery. Conditions that are not consistent with effective service are reported.

These conditions are documented as non-conformities, incidents, patient care committee, or medical staff peer review reports. A non-conformity is defined as a non-fulfillment of a requirement related to an intended or specified use. An incident is defined as any event that is not consistent with normal patient care or employee/visitor safety that either did, or could, directly result in bodily injury, or alter the planned course of treatment.

Boston IVF

ISO 9001:2000
QUALITY SYSTEMS MANUAL

QM
Page 28 of 32
Issued: Initial Draft
Revised: 12/28/04
Supersedes: N/A

Boston IVF maintains a system to monitor, detect and correct non-conformities.

The patient complaint reporting committee monitors patient complaints and incidents.

Every employee has the responsibility for identification and reporting of non-conformities. Reviews of non-conformities are maintained as part of Quality Records.

Any employee has the authority and responsibility to stop and/or correct service non-conformities found not to meet applicable standards and to report the event.

Documented processes cover:

- Identification and reporting of occurrences

- Parameters for correcting and/or discontinuing/revising non-conforming practice

- Records of occurrences/non-conformities

- Medical staff practice reviews (transfusion, transfer, mortality, etc.).

Non-conforming material (medical supplies) is segregated, marked or tagged, and dispositioned.

8.4   Analysis of data

In order to verify the effectiveness of services provided by Boston IVF, controlled activities affecting the quality of service and the effective monitoring of the Quality System, ensures the continuous improvement of services. Boston IVF documents a procedure that outlines how data is collected and generated by measuring and monitoring activities for a variety of services provided by the Center.

Information regarding the following topics is analyzed:

- Customer satisfaction

- Quality indicators (conformity to process requirements, trends of processes)

- Opportunities for preventive action

- Suppliers

Top Management is charged with the responsibility of selecting suitable statistical methods and also identifying which data will be collected, analyzed and utilized in conjunction with any continual improvement efforts.

Boston IVF

ISO 9001:2000
QUALITY SYSTEMS MANUAL

QM
Page 29 of 32
Issued: Initial Draft
Revised: 12/28/04
Supersedes: N/A

8.5   Improvement

8.5.1 Planning for continual improvement

Boston IVF continually improves the quality management system through the use of the Quality Policy, quality objectives, internal audit program, corrective/preventive action systems and management reviews.

8.5.2 Corrective action

Boston IVF maintains a documented procedure defining requirements for reviewing non-conformities, determining their cause(s), evaluating the need for action to prevent recurrence, determining and implementing the action, recording the results, and reviewing the corrective action taken to determine its effectiveness.

Corrective actions are appropriate to the effects of the non-conformities.

8.5.3 Preventive action

Boston IVF maintains a documented procedure defining requirements for eliminating the causes of potential non-conformities.

The procedure defines the method for determining potential non-conformities and their cause(s), evaluating the need for action to prevent occurrence, determining and implementing the action needed, recording the results, and reviewing the preventive action taken to determine its effectiveness.

Preventive actions are appropriate to the effects of the potential non-conformities.

Processes and relevant issues that may potentially cause non-conformities are identified and systematically reviewed as part of the preventive action program.

To eliminate potential causes of non-conformities in the Quality System, Boston IVF analyzes:

- Processes
- Trends in non-conformance
- Outcome measurement reports
- Results of changes implemented in response to preventive action plans

All employees have the opportunity to identify the need for a preventive action plan. Members of the Self-Directed Leadership Teams initiate preventive action plans as appropriate.

Procedures document the steps involved in addressing circumstances that warrant preventive action. Preventive actions are recorded and reviewed as a part of Management Review.

ISO 9001:2000
QUALITY SYSTEMS MANUAL

QM
Page 30 of 32
Issued: Initial Draft
Revised: 12/28/04
Supersedes: N/A

ADDENDUM 1: BOSTON IVF System Procedures

ISO 2000	System Procedure#	Title
5.1		N/A See Quality Manual
5.2		N/A See Quality Manual
5.3		N/A See Quality Manual
5.4.1		N/A See Quality Manual
5.4.2		BOSTON IVF Annual Planning/Strategic Planning
5.5.2		N/A See Quality Manual, attached Organizational Chart
5.5.3		N/A See Quality Manual
5.5.4		N/A See Quality Manual
5.5.5		N/A See Quality Manual
5.5.6	P01.601L	BOSTON IVF Control of Documents
5.5.7*		BOSTON IVF Control of Quality Records
5.6.1		BOSTON IVF Annual Planning/Strategic Planning
5.6.2		
6.1		BOSTON IVF Budget Process
6.2.1		Centralized Physician Credentialing
		BOSTON IVF Hiring Process
6.2.2*		BOSTON IVF Education and Training of Employees
6.3		(All systems documents)
6.4		
7.1		(All systems documents)
		BOSTON IVF Preservation of Supplies
		BOSTON IVF Continuous Improvement Procedure
7.2.1	67.P20	BOSTON IVF Continuous Improvement Procedure
7.2.2	P17.10	Verification of Orders
7.2.3		
7.3.1		BOSTON IVF Design of Plans of Care
7.3.2		BOSTON IVF Design of Plans of Care
7.3.3		BOSTON IVF Design of Plans of Care

ISO 9001:2000
QUALITY SYSTEMS MANUAL

QM
Page 31 of 32

Issued: Initial Draft
Revised: 12/28/04
Supersedes: N/A

Boston IVF

7.3.4		BOSTON IVF Design of Plans of Care
7.3.5		BOSTON IVF Design of Plans of Care
7.3.6		BOSTON IVF Design of Plans of Care
7.3.7		BOSTON IVF Design of Plans of Care
7.4.1		BOSTON IVF Purchasing
7.4.2		BOSTON IVF Purchasing
7.4.3		BOSTON IVF Purchasing
7.5.1		BOSTON IVF Operations Control
7.5.2		BOSTON IVF ID and Traceability
7.5.3	42.P01	BOSTON IVF Patient/Resident Personal Property and Valuables
7.5.4		BOSTON IVF Preservation of Supplies
7.5.5		BOSTON IVF Validating Special Processes
7.6	P17.P118	Calibration of Equipment BOSTON IVF Control of Measuring and Monitoring Devices
8.1	P67.P20	BOSTON IVF Continuous Improvement Procedure
8.2.1		
8.2.2*	P01.602	BOSTON IVF Internal Audits
8.2.3	67.P20	BOSTON IVF Continuous Improvement Procedure
		Key Process Document
8.2.4	67.P20	BOSTON IVF Continuous Improvement Procedure
		BOSTON IVF Annual Planning/Strategic Planning
8.3*		
8.4	67.P20	BOSTON IVF Continuous Improvement Procedure
8.5.1	67.P20	BOSTON IVF Continuous Improvement Procedure
8.5.2*	67.P20	BOSTON IVF Continuous Improvement Procedure
8.5.3*	67.P20	BOSTON IVF Continuous Improvement Procedure

* Identifies Procedures REQUIRED for this element

Policy/Principle (Purpose of document control)

Documents are used to control activities in the company by defining the method for doing tasks correctly. Those important tasks that should be done the same way consistently are defined in the documents.

Documents that control activities must themselves be controlled:

- To be sure that the correct version of the document is in use;
- To ensure that each document that is used to control an activity has been reviewed and approved by an authority before it is released for use;
- To know that documents are available where they are needed.

NOTE: It is important that written documentation and actual practice match. In review of existing documents, watch for opportunities to simplify and eliminate overlapping and redundant paperwork.

Responsibility

All employees

Procedure

Definition of controlled documents and authorization

All documents are approved (authorized) by the appropriate authority before use.

Type of document	Authorized by
Quality Manual	
This manual describes the operating system at Boston IVF. It is a policy book, and is numbered the same as the ISO 9001-2000 standard to show that each standard is met.	COO, Medical Director
System Procedure (SP)	
Every employee at Boston IVF follows these procedures. They are located in the MR (Management Representative) folder in the Boston IVF documents.	MR
Procedure (P)	
Policies and Procedures (P&Ps) that describe how to do the work in each department. Located in the department folder in Boston IVF documents.	Appropriate Supervisor

continued

continued

Work Instruction (WI)

Detailed, stepwise instructions for one task or a quick reference designed for daily use. Usually linked to a procedure, to further explain an activity. Note: if a form is used and the form makes it obvious how to complete it, no further instruction is necessary.

Appropriate Supervisor

Form (F)

Forms may be a fill-in-the-blank document or a document that needs control only to identify the current copy of the document. Forms are records of activities or contain the records once they have been filled out. Examples of forms that are not filled out are Employee Handbooks, the Quality Policy statement, brochures used for Marketing activities.

Appropriate Supervisor

Job Description (JD)

Description of the responsibilities and authority for each position at Boston IVF.

Appropriate Supervisor

Location and accessibility of controlled documents

Controlled documents are electronic and located in the Boston IVF Documents folder (Path: H drive\Boston IVF folder\IVF company folder\Department folder). Control means that only the current document is available. Access to folders, for changing documents, and electronic signatures is controlled and defined in the IT system by the system administrator. Electronic format also ensures legibility of documents.

Identification of controlled documents

The Quality Manual (QM), System Procedures (SP), Procedures (P), Job descriptions (JD) and Work Instructions (WI) are identified by: Boston IVF Logo, the type of document, the title, a control number, revision level, and page numbers (in format "page x of y") in the header of the document. Forms are identified by their number and Rev. level located in the lower right corner.

Templates are used to generate system documents and to control the format for each type of document. Click on the link to view the templates.

System Procedure Template
Procedure Template
Work Instruction Template
Form Template
Job Description Template

Control numbers are constructed as follows:

AB-CD-##, where
AB = kind of document (QM, SP, P, WI, JD or F)
CD = department designation
= number assigned by the Management Representative or department supervisor.

Department designations are as follows:

Designation	DEPARTMENT	Designation	DEPARTMENT
MR	Management Representative	MD	Physicians
EL	Endocrine Lab	MB	Mind/Body
AE	Andrology/ Embryology Lab	BL	Billing
US	Ultrasound	FN	Financial
OR	OR/PACU	IT	IT
ON	Office Nursing	HR	HR
MK	Marketing	CL	Clerical
IN	IVF Nursing	BE	Building and Equipment
		DE	Data Entry

Creating or changing controlled documents

Documents that are numbered as defined in this procedure can be changed at any time, as long as the changes follow the correct path. Change authorization is defined in the IT system. Most employees have 'view only' authorization. These employees may suggest changes to the authorizer (Department Supervisor) but cannot make the changes themselves.

Boston IVF

SYSTEMS PROCEDURE

Document and Data Control

Approved by: MR

SP-MR-01
Revision: 2
Page 4 of 6

All work is performed in accordance with the documents. This ISO statement means that when a procedure, work instruction or form is changed either the reason the change needs to be made is to bring the document into line with what is already happening, or the people who do the work described must be trained to do the new things that were changed. In either case, communication is important. Be sure that everyone knows about changes that affect their work.

New documents and changes to documents must be authorized; see the table on pages 1 & 2 for the authorizing authority.

Editorial changes (spelling, spacing, punctuation) are not changes to the content of the document, and can be made and saved at any time without a record of a new revision.

All documents follow the same general path, as follows:

- Create/change the document/template header and footer – name, revision level, authorizer; remove form # from the template
- Create/change the body of the document
- Get authorization
- Complete the Review and Revision History section
- Save in the appropriate location
- Revise the appropriate document list
- Communicate the changes

For specific steps, follow the appropriate Work Instruction, as follows:

WI-MR-01 – How to Create a Procedure

WI-MR-02 – How to Review/Change a Procedure

WI-MR-03 – How to Create a Form

WI-MR-04 – How to Review/Change a Form

WI-MR-05 – How to Create a Work Instruction

WI-MR-06 – How to Review/Change a Work Instruction

Job Descriptions: See the WIs for Forms–Use the Job Description template.

Availability at point of use

Documents are available at all times on the server. Any employee has access to view them from his/her computer terminal.

Printed copies of procedures are not controlled and may only be printed with authorization by the appropriate departmental supervisor. Reasons for printing procedures may include: preparing revisions and training new employees. Printed copies must be destroyed as soon as the task or training is completed.

External documents

External documents are identified as documents in use at Boston IVF that are not generated and controlled within the company. Examples: applicable statutes, standards, requisition forms, insurance forms, equipment manuals, etc.

Reference materials are distinguished from external documents in the system by marking the material or its location (shelf, bookcase, etc.) "Reference".

The department supervisor is responsible for external documents in use in his/her department. The documents are listed on the department External Document list along with the person responsible or the location of the document.

Upon receipt of new or updated versions of requirements, the appropriate supervisor reviews the requirements and/or the changes to them. (S)He is responsible to discuss changes with the staff who have need of the information.

Obsolete documents

An obsolete document is one that has been replaced by a new version: old copies of documents that have been changed.

Obsolete document are marked "Obsolete" clearly on the first page. If an obsolete document has multiple pages and it is likely that individual pages may become separated from the rest of the document, each page is also marked with a single mark across the whole page with a highlighter pen.

Boston IVF

Review and Revision History

Revision Number	Authorized Signature(s)	Date	Description of change (If no changes, write N/A)

Policy/Principle

Records are defined as information that shows that requirements stated any-where in the quality management system have been met. (The form itself is a document under document control – this system procedure addresses the infor-mation that appears in various formats such as on forms, in databases, in reports, etc.)

Information that constitutes a record is defined or identified and must be readable; methods for storage of records show how each record is indexed so that an individual record can be found. This control of records procedure defines controls for identification, storage, protection, retrieval, retention time, and disposition of records.

Responsibility

All employees follow this System Procedure.

Department Supervisors can request additions, deletions or changes to the Record Log.

The Management Representative (MR) or designee is responsible to main-tain the Record Log.

Procedure

Identification of records

Records are listed by title or type of record on the Record Log in accordance with requirements from System Procedures, Procedures, and Work Instructions. When a record is maintained on a form, the title of the record matches the title of the form.

Indexing, storage, retrieval, retention

The Record Log identifies:

> Title/Description (Title of document/file/database – may be a descriptive phrase)
>
> Location (Be specific if onsite – example, HR office)
>
> Department (See SP-MR-01 for listing)
>
> Disposal (Method such as discard or shred)
>
> Responsible (Appropriate Department Supervisor)
>
> Access and retrieval (how they are filed: by customer name, by date, etc.)
>
> Minimum Retention time.

Protection and disposition

Records are filed in hard copy format or are located in databases electronically. Adequate backups ensure the security of electronic data, and limited access to hard copy files (only company employees within the appropriate department, the MR, and internal auditors) protects hard copies. Medical Records and other confidential records are safeguarded against inappropriate access.

Records whose retention time is over may be discarded or destroyed. Method for disposition (discard or destroy by shredding) is identified on the Record Log, held by the Management Representative. Confidential records must be destroyed at the end of the retention period.

Issuance of Records – Medical Release of Information

To ensure a rapid and legal release of all medical information that may be pertinent to the health care of a patient, the following procedure will be followed:

1. If a patient needs to have their medical information released either to them or to another provider, a RELEASE OF INFORMATION AUTHORIZATION Form must be completed by the patient.
2. Once the patient has signed this authorization form, the information may then be mailed to the 3rd party or released to the patient.
3. Place the signed authorization form in the patient's file.

Medical Records – Contents, Timely Completion, Purging and Archiving

It is the policy of Boston IVF that all medical records are completed in a timely manner and contain essential information. Records may be purged from the active files and forwarded for long-term archiving after inactive status of at least 6 months.

1. The medical record will contain the patient registration with signed consent for treatment, nurse's notes, physician's notes or dictation, Return To Work Certificate, test results and patient discharge instructions. The record may also contain insurance carrier inquiries, correspondence related to the case and administrative notes. The record shall not include drug screen results.
2. Nurses and physicians notes are completed within 24 hours of treatment.
3. Medical records are maintained in the active file in the Business Health Clinic after the patient has been discharged for such time as specified by the Medical Director or Case Manager. Retaining the record after

discharge allows for clarification of return to work status and insurance carrier inquiries.

4. After the record is no longer needed by the Business health clinic, the record is purged from the Business Health active file and forwarded to the Finley Medical Records Department for long-term storage.

Adding/removing from the Record Log

To change the Record Log, the department supervisor notifies the MR via email of the request for change. When the change involves a change in the use of forms (add or drop), follow the document control conventions in the System Procedure for Document and Data Control.

The MR revises the Log, changes the revision level, and archives the old Log. Only the current Record Log is available for use on the server.

Change History

Revision	Responsibility	Page(s)	Nature of change

Document Authorization

_____   _____
Authorized Signature   Date

_____   _____
Authorized Signature   Date

Policy/Principle

A non-conformance is defined as a non-fulfillment of a requirement. It is any problem or occurrence that is not consistent with the routine operation of Boston IVF. This may include, but is not limited to: non-fulfillment of a quality objective, patient complaints, problems with patient samples or gametes, patient identification, equipment problems, paperwork problems and out of range QC values.

Boston IVF monitors, detects and corrects non-conformities. Non-conformities may be identified by many methods. Activities involving assessment, monitoring, completing checklists, and simply performing daily tasks in accordance with established procedures are all opportunities to fulfill requirements. Any non-fulfillment of a requirement is a non-conformance and is reported. Reporting is by exception; records of meeting requirements are kept by established reporting formats throughout the system, with non-conformities reported to the Non-conformance Database. Non-conformities include incidents and patient complaints.

A correction is an action taken to correct a non-conformance. If possible, the employee who reports the non-conformance should correct the problem.

Departmental supervisors are to be notified of all non-conformities that occur in their department and they are responsible for corrective action and all follow-up. Follow-up may include communicating with physicians, the patient advocate, the MR, the patient reporting group and the COO. The departmental supervisor is responsible for ensuring that all non-conformance reports are completed up to the point of corrective action which is the MR's responsibility.

Corrective action is required when the non-conformance is serious enough, or has occurred often enough, to require further action beyond the immediate correction. Corrective action is also taken when a quality objective has not been met; see the departmental quality objectives list.

Responsibility

All employees are responsible to comply with established requirements; all employees are also responsible to identify and report non-conforming events or conditions wherever they exist.

Any employee has the authority and responsibility to stop and/or correct non-conformities (an activity found not to meet applicable standards) and to report the event.

All departmental supervisors are responsible for reviewing all departmental non-conformance reports, identifying and notifying appropriate Boston IVF personnel (i.e. other departmental supervisors, physicians, the patient advocate, etc.), and following up on each report until the report is complete.

Boston IVF

SYSTEMS PROCEDURE

Control of Non-conformity

Approved by:	SP-MR-04
COO	Revision: 0
MR	Page 2 of 4

Procedure

Employee procedure

When a non-conformance is identified, the identifying employee is responsible for appropriate first response. The immediate concern is to correct or eliminate the non-conforming condition including notifying the immediate supervisor as appropriate. When specific protocols/procedures exist for response and reporting, they are to be followed.

The appropriate supervisor is responsible to review the report. When the original reporter leaves blank entry fields, the supervisor completes any additional information that is required. These identifiers make searches and reports possible from the database. The supervisor determines whether further action is warranted. Further action may be additional actions to correct the non-conformance, designation as an incident, and/or identifying the need for Corrective Action.

Stepwise procedure for reporting a non-conformance:

1. Double click on the FileMaker Pro icon on your desktop.
2. Click on "Hosts" and then double click on Non-conformance database.
3. Enter the password "report" when prompted.
4. Follow the instructions on the first screen and you will reach a second screen entitled "Employee report of Non-conformance/correction".
5. Enter the type of non-conformance from the list. If it is not on the list, choose "other". Enter the date of the occurrence, your department and your supervisor.
6. Describe the non-conformance, in detail, in the box labeled "Description of nonconformance". Include the name(s), DOB(s) and DOR(s) of any patient(s) and names of other employees or supervisors who may have been involved.
7. If you corrected the non-conformance, please describe the correction in the "Correction of non-conformance" box. If there was no correction performed, enter N/A.
8. Enter your name and signature at the bottom.
9. Prior to clicking in the box to exit the program, re-read your report to be sure that you have included all the appropriate details. Note the Report ID # so you can include that number in your email to your supervisor.
10. Click in the indicated box and you will automatically exit the program.
11. As soon as possible, email or telephone your supervisor to inform him/her of the non-conformance and be sure to include the Report ID #.

Supervisory procedure

1. You are notified of a non-conformance.

2. Double click on the FileMaker Pro icon on your desktop.

3. Click on "Hosts" and then double click on Non-conformance database.

4. Enter the password "xxxxxxx" when prompted.

5. When the file opens, click on the Layout pop-up menu (bar in the upper left hand corner of the screen, just below the word "File"). The list that appears contains the layouts (screens) which can be viewed.

6. Click on "Report of non-conformance (supervisor copy)" and the report layout will open. This layout is a copy of the information that the employee completed and includes a description of the non-conformance and any correction that was taken.

7. Next, click on the Layout pop-up menu again and click on the Supervisor correction report layout (you can return to the "Report of non-conformance (supervisor copy)" anytime).

8. Complete this layout by filling in each field (box) in the layout.

9. "Physician performed correction?" (if yes, complete the name of physician field), "Pt. advocate performed correction?", "COO performed correction?", "Medical Director performed correction?" If you contacted one of these managers to perform the correction (i.e. a patient needed to be called regarding a problem), write "yes", otherwise "no". Even if someone else performed the correction, you are responsible for ensuring that either (s)he or you completes the report.

10. If the non-conformance is related to a quality objective, write "yes" in the appropriate field and indicate which objective.

11. Describe the correction. If the correction taken by the employee who reported the non-conformance was sufficient, be sure to indicate that in this field.

12. Print and sign your name and date.

13. If you informed the patient reporting committee, indicate "yes" in the appropriate field.

14. If Corrective action is required, write "yes" in the "corrective action required field".

15. Refer to System Procedure SP-MR-05 Corrective Action.

16. Inform the MR that there is corrective action required.

Quality Objective Reports

When a quality objective non-conformance is reported, follow the procedure above, except that the supervisor begins the report on the Report of Non-conformance (supervisor's copy) instead of the employee's copy. Write "yes" in the "related to quality objective" field and write which quality objective in the "which objective?" field.

Change History

Revision	Responsibility	Page(s)	Nature of change

Document Authorization

Authorized Signature	Date
Authorized Signature	Date

Policy/Principle

These activities are the method for problem solving and continuous improvement. Boston IVF defines requirements for reviewing non-conformities, determining their cause(s), evaluating the need for action to prevent recurrence, determining and implementing the action, recording the results, and reviewing the corrective action taken to determine its effectiveness.

Corrective actions are appropriate to the effects of the non-conformities.

Corrective actions differ from corrections of non-conformities in that the corrective action is initiated to find and resolve the root cause of the problem.

Responsibility

All employees are responsible to know and follow this procedure.

The Management Representative (MR) tracks Corrective Actions to completion, sending reminders to the appropriate person when a deadline is approaching or overdue. The MR reports on the status of corrective actions to the ISO Committee and to top management.

Department Heads bear primary responsibility for corrective action, designating responsibility as appropriate and overseeing timely response.

Procedure

Who initiates corrective action

Non-conformities are identified and reported in accordance with SP-MR-04. Supervisors and/or the ISO Committee review non-conformance reports periodically to determine the need for Corrective Action based on non-conformance trends and the effect of the non-conformity.

Corrective Action is initiated immediately by the person who reports the non-conformity when:

- The non-conformance impacts employee or patient safety

- The non-conformance is a serious patient complaint or any serious event

How to start the process

Initiate corrective action by selecting "yes" in the Corrective Action needed on the appropriate screen in the non-conformance database. Email the department head with the non-conformance number.

Completing the corrective action

1. The department head reviews the non-conformance, and the correction already undertaken.

2. (S)He

   - Assigns a team or an individual to investigate the root cause of the problem (can be themselves);

   - Inputs this information to the appropriate field in the non-conformance database in the corrective action screen;

   - Notifies them of the assignment and when it is due;

   - Inputs due dates;

   - Attaches electronic signature to complete the first section for corrective action.

3. The designee(s) complete their investigation of the root cause and input the information to the proper section of the corrective action screen.

4. The designee(s) determine, document and implement an action plan. Sign and date the section and notify the MR that the corrective action is in place.

5. The MR

   - Reviews the record

   - Assigns a person or audit team to evaluate whether the action was effective

   - Assigns a due date for the evaluation

6. After the evaluation is performed, the evidence of effective implementation is documented, signed and dated to close the corrective action. If the investigation results in a conclusion that the action was not effective, the department head and the MR are notified, the record completed to show the action is not closed, and the investigation of root cause resumed. Follow the same steps, above.

Change History

Revision	Responsibility	Page(s)	Nature of change

Document Authorization

_____   _____

Authorized Signature   Date

_____   _____

Authorized Signature   Date

Policy/Principle

Preventive actions prevent potential non-conformities, providing a means for improvement that is independent from solving problems.

Responsibility

All employees are responsible to know and follow this procedure.

The Management Representative (MR) tracks Preventive Actions to completion, sending reminders to the appropriate person when a deadline is approaching or overdue. The MR reports on the status of preventive actions to the ISO Committee and to top management.

The MR and top management bear primary responsibility for preventive action, designating responsibility as appropriate and overseeing timely response.

Procedure

Who initiates preventive action

All employees have the opportunity to identify the need for a preventive action plan.

To eliminate potential causes of non-conformities in the Quality System, the ISO Committee analyzes:

- Processes
- Trends in non-conformance
- Outcome measurement reports
- Results of changes implemented in response to preventive action plans and may initiate preventive actions.

How to start and complete the process

1. Access the preventive action database and complete all fields on the first screen.
2. The Management Representative and/or a member of top management reviews the preventive action presented and determines a response, completing the Response section. When the response is to develop an action plan, a team or person is assigned.
3. The designee(s) determine, document and implement an action plan. Sign and date the section and notify the MR that the preventive action is in place.

4. The MR
   - Reviews the record
   - Assigns a person or audit team to evaluate whether the action was effective
   - Assigns a due date for the evaluation

5. After the evaluation is performed, the evidence of effective implementation is documented, signed and dated to close the preventive action. If the investigation results in a conclusion that the action was not effective, the department head and the MR are notified, the record completed to show the action is not closed, and the plan is revisited and revised. Follow the same steps, as shown above.

SYSTEMS PROCEDURE

Preventive Action

Boston IVF

Approved by:	SP-MR-06
COO	Revision: 0
MR	Page 3 of 3

Change History

Revision	Responsibility	Page(s)	Nature of change

Document Authorization

_____   _____
Authorized Signature   Date

_____   _____
Authorized Signature   Date

Policy/Principle

The company carries out comprehensive and systematic internal audits to determine the effectiveness of the quality system and to verify whether activities comply with the planned arrangements.

Responsibility

All employees are responsible to cooperate with the internal auditors and to respond to any non-conformances identified.

Internal auditors are responsible to perform internal audits on schedule and to submit audit reports without delay.

The Management Representative has overall responsibility for the internal audit system.

Responsibilities are as follows:

- Schedule audits along with any rescheduling that is necessary
- Select auditors, define auditees
- Communicate the audit schedule to all concerned
- Ensure personnel performing audits are independent of the area audited
- Ensure that audit activities are carried out
- Review and report on audit results to management

Procedure

Internal audit schedule

Each year the Management Representative prepares the annual Quality System Audits Schedule. The audit schedule is based on the degree of importance of the activities. The schedule requires that both the processes and the ISO standard are audited over the course of each year.

Internal auditors

The Management Representative selects trained auditor(s) to carry out the audit. Auditors are independent of the area being audited. No auditor audits their own work.

Audit method

A checklist is prepared by the auditor(s) using the department documents and the ISO 9001-2000 standard. Previous audit reports for the department under audit may be used in preparation of the checklist.

SYSTEMS PROCEDURE

Internal Audits

Approved by:	SP-MR-07
COO	Revision: 0
MR	Page 2 of 3

Boston IVF

During the audit, the auditor(s) document any non-conformances on corrective action requests (CARs). A copy of each CAR is given to the Department Head at the end of the audit. The auditor keeps the original CAR, which is submitted to the MR along with the checklist, any notes, and an Audit Summary as the audit report. Audit reports are due to the MR within one day after the audit has been performed.

The responsible staff is responsible to complete the corrective action according to the agreed date on the CAR.

The audit report is followed-up and endorsed by the auditors. Management Representative or responsible auditor then reviews the completeness and effectiveness of the corrective action.

Workflow

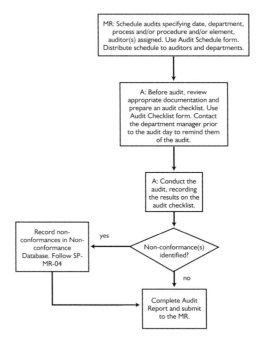

Change History

Revision	*Responsibility*	*Page(s)*	*Nature of change*

Document Authorization

Authorized Signature   Date

Authorized Signature   Date

Sample Process Flow Charts

This appendix contains a sample of various flow charts or process maps. The samples that follow are provided to allow the health-care organization to understand more clearly what is meant by the ISO 9001:2000 phrase 'sequence and interaction' of related processes discussed in various chapters of this book. Additionally, these charts and maps will assist in determining how to depict them correctly as the health-care provider begins the implementation process toward ISO 9001:2000 registration. It should be noted that the these flow charts and process maps alone will not be enough for the health-care organization to meet all of the requirements of the ISO 9001:2000 standard nor will certification be granted by simply editing these documents and using them. The charts and maps are examples only and provide a starting point for the organization.

It is highly recommended that assistance from qualified consultants be sought prior to actual creation of work flows and process maps. When seeking guidance from consultants the health-care organization should consider two important factors: 1) that the firm providing consultation is ISO 9001:2000 certified themselves, and 2) that the firm has worked with other health-care organization assisting them achieve ISO 9001:2000 certification.

HUMAN RESOURCES PROCESS

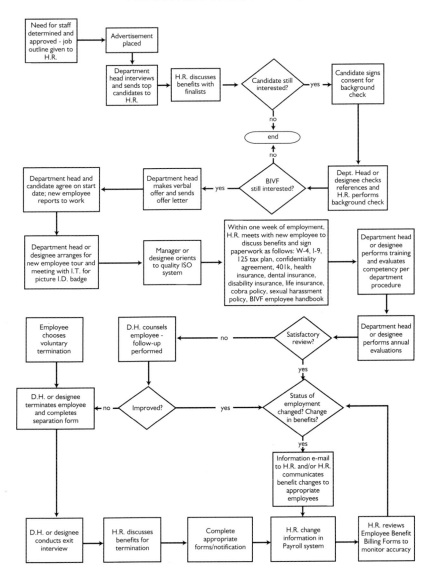

PRACTICE/CLINICAL TELEPHONE PROCESS

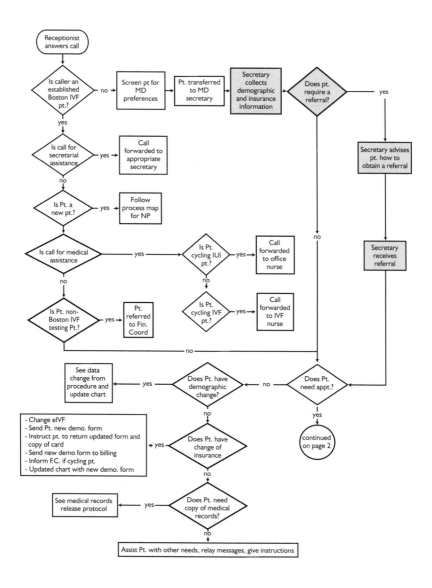

PRACTICE/CLINICAL TELEPHONE PROCESS

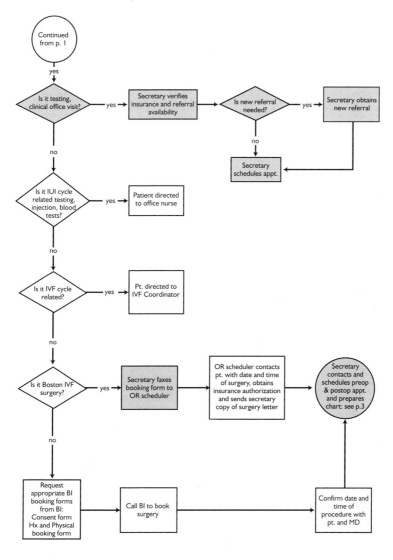

ART FLOW SHEET – IVF NURSING

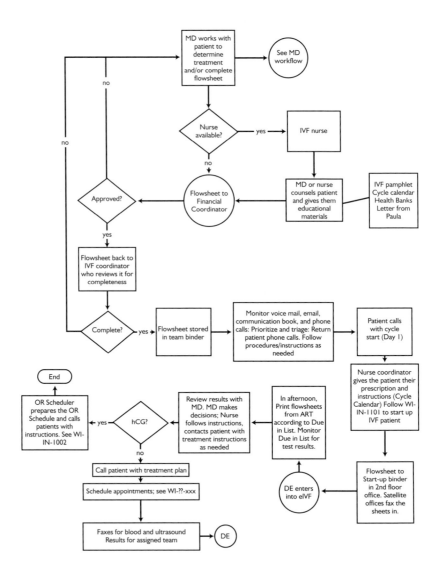

OFFICE NURSING PROCESS MAP

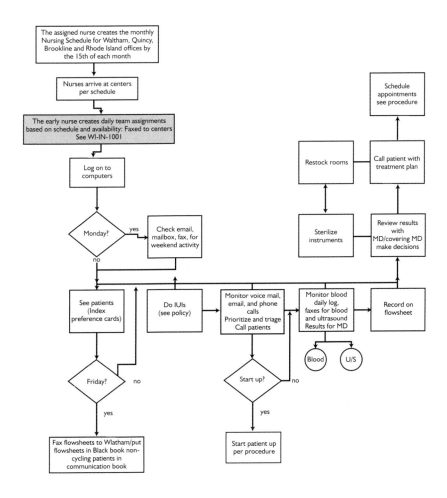

Index

accountability 54
audit *see* internal audit
authority 54

calibration 61, 78–79
Clauses 0-2: scope, normative references and definitions 20
Clause 3: terms and definitions 20–24
Clause 4: quality management system requirements 12, 18, 24–45
  4.1: general requirements 24–25
  4.2: documentation requirements 25–29
    4.2.1a: quality policy, goals and objectives 29–30
    4.2.1c: quality system level procedures 36–41
    4.2.1e: records 41
    4.2.2: quality manual 30–36
    4.2.3: control of documents 41–44
    4.2.4: control of records 44–45
Clause 5: management responsibility 12, 18, 46–58
  5.1: management commitment 46
  5.2: customer focus 47–47
  5.3: quality policy 49
  5.4: planning 50–54

    5.4.1: quality objectives 50–52
    5.4.2: quality management system planning 52–53
  5.5: responsibility, authority and communication 54–55
    5.5.1: responsibility and authority 54
    5.5.2: management representative 54–55
    5.5.3: internal communication 55
  5.6: management review 55–58
    5.6.2: management review input 56–57
    5.6.3: management review output 57
Clause 6: resource management 12, 18, 59–63
  6.3: infrastructure 60–62
  6.4: work environment 60–62
Clause 7: product and service realization 12, 18, 64–79
  7.1: planning of service delivery 64–65
  7.2: customer-related processes 65–67
    7.2.1: determination of customer requirements 65–66

7.2.1: review of customer requirements 65–66

7.2.3: customer communication 67

7.3: design and development 67–70

7.4: purchasing 70–72

7.4.1: purchasing process 70

7.4.2: evaluation of vendors and subcontractors 70–71

7.4.3: verification of purchased product 71–72

7.5: production and service provision 72–78

7.5.1: control of operations 72–76

7.5.2: validation of processes 76

7.5.3: identification and traceability 76–77

7.5.4: customer property 77

7.5.5: preservation of product 78

7.6: measurement and monitoring devices 78–79

Clause 8: measurement, analysis and improvement 12, 18, 80–90

8.2.1: customer satisfaction 80–81

8.2.2: internal audit 81–86

8.2.3/8.2.4: measuring and monitoring of processes and products 86

8.3: control of non-conformity 87–88

8.4: analysis of data 88

8.5.1: continual improvement 88–89

8.5.2: corrective action 89–90

8.5.3: preventive action 89–90

clinical processes 6–7

see also process management approach

communication

internal communication 55

of quality policy 49

with customers 67

continual improvement 11, 74, 88–89

process improvement 8–9

control 72–73

of documents 41–44, 147–152

of non-conformity 87–88, 157–160

of operations 72–76

of records 44–45, 153–156

corrective action 89–90, 161–163

credentialing 62–63

customer 2–3, 22–23, 47–48

communication with 67

customer focus 2–3, 47–48

customer property 23, 77

customer requirements 48

determination of relating to service delivery 65–66

review of 24, 65–66

customer satisfaction 3, 80–81

data analysis 88

decision-making

employee involvement 5–6

factual approach 11–12

design 67–70

validation 69

verification 69

development 67–70

documentation requirements 25–29

control of documents 41–44, 147–152

documents of external origin 44

forms control 44

quality manual 30–36

sample manual 115–146

quality policy, goals and objectives 29–30

quality system level procedures 36–41

procedure writing format 39–40

quality plan 40
work instructions 41
records 41
    control of 44–45, 153–156
documented procedures 26–27,
30–31, 37
see also documentation
    requirements
documents 26, 27
    control of 41–44, 147–152
        documents of external origin 44
        forms control 44
    planning output documents 54
    referenced documents 44
    see also documentation
        requirements

employee involvement 5–6
equipment
    calibration 61, 78–79
    preventive maintenance 60–61

factual approach to decision-making
11–12
fertility services
    general requirements 24–25
    service delivery 22, 24–25
    see also quality management system
flow charts 74–76
    samples 170–175
forms control 44

Hoshin planning 50

identification 76–77
infrastructure 60–62
internal audit 81–86, 167–169
    auditor's responsibilities 83
    definition 81–82
    human aspects 83–86
    purpose of auditing 82–83
internal communication 55

ISO (International Standardization
    Organization) 14–15
ISO 9000 series 14, 15–16
    re-structuring and consolidation of
        16–17
ISO 9000:2000 17
ISO 9001 17–19
ISO 9001:2000 1–2
    comparison with MBNQA 91–95
    self-assessment instrument 96–113
    see also quality management
        system; *specific clauses*
ISO 9004:2000 17–19
IVF practice
    service delivery 2, 13, 24–25
    see also fertility services; quality
        management system

leadership 3–5

Malcolm Baldrige National Quality
    Award (MBNQA) 91–95
management
    commitment 46
    system approach 10
    top management 3
    see also Clause 5: management
        responsibility; process
        management approach; quality
        management system
management representative 54–55
management review 55–58
    input 56–57
    output 57
    records 58
MBNQA 91–95
measurement 78–79
    of processes and products 86
medical policies and procedures 24
medical record 24
monitoring
    devices 78–79

of processes and products 86

non-conformity 23–24
  control of 87–88, 157–160
Nursing Care Plan 69

operational planning 53
operations, control of 72–76

patient 22–23
  see also customer
planning 50–54
  Hoshin planning 50
  operational planning 53
  output documents 54
  quality management system
    planning 52–53
  quality objectives 50–52
  service delivery 64–65
  strategic planning 53
  tools 50
practice chart 54
preservation of product 78
preventive action 89–90, 164–166
privileging 62–63
procedures 24, 36–41
  documented procedures 26–27,
    30–31, 37
  quality plan 40
  work instructions 41
  writing 38–39
    format 39–40
process management approach 1–2,
  6–10, 13, 72–76
  continual process improvement
    8–9, 74
  process model 7–8
  see also quality management system
processes 22, 74
  measuring and monitoring of 86
  purchasing process 70
  validation of 76

see also process management
  approach
product 21–22
  measuring and monitoring of
    86–87
  preservation of 78
  see also Clause 7: product and
    service realization
property, of customers 23, 77
proprietary information 32
purchasing 70–72
  evaluation of vendors and
    subcontractors 70–71
  process of 70
  verification of purchased product
    71–72

quality documentation 8
quality management system 1–13
  continual improvement 11, 74,
    88–89
  customer focus 2–3
  documentation 26
  factual approach to decision-
    making 11–12
  involvement of people 5–6
  leadership 3–5
  mutually beneficial supplier
    relationships 12
  planning 52–53
  system approach 10
  see also Clause 4: quality
    management system
    requirements; process
    management approach
quality manual 30–36
  contents of 34–36
  data collection 33
  page format 32
  preparation 31–32
  proprietary information 32
  responsibility for 33

responsibility section 33
sample manual 115–146
writing 33–34
quality objectives 29–30
planning 50–52
quality plan 40, 52–53
see also planning
quality policy 29–30, 49, 51

records 41
control of 44–45, 153–156
of management review 58
referenced documents 44
requirements 28–29
documentation requirements
25–29
general requirements 24–25
see also customer requirements
resource management 12, 18, 59–63
infrastructure 60–62
work environment 60–62
responsibility 54
of auditors 83

self-assessment instrument 96–113
service 21–22
service delivery 2, 13

determination of customer
requirements 65–66
fertility service delivery 22, 24–25
planning 64–65
see also Clause 7: product and
service realization
strategic planning 53
subcontractor evaluation 70–71
supplier relationships 12
see also vendors
system 22
system approach 10

terms and definitions 20–24
traceability 76–77

validation
of design 69
of processes 76
vendors 70
evaluation of 70–71
supplier relationships 12
verification
of design 69
of purchased product 71–72

work environment 60–62
work instructions 31, 41